DEVOTIONALS FOR TWO MONTHS

SEPTEMBER AND OCTOBER

Leslie M. John

These devotionals for two months are part of series of Devotionals for a year.

ISBN: 978-0-9907801-1-3

Vol. 5

Contents

DEVOTIONALS FOR TWO MONTHS....1

SEPTEMBER AND OCTOBER....1

Leslie M. John....1

PREFACE....7

SEPTEMBER DEVOTIONALS....10

DAY 1 STORMS CALMED DOWN....11

DAY 2 JESUS CASTS OUT DEVILS....15

DAY 3 ALMIGHTY GOD AND HIS POWER....18

DAY 4 DAY OF ATONEMENT....22

DAY 5 STRIVING WITH MAN....25

DAY 6 SIN AMONG ROMANS....28

DAY 7 PARALYTIC HEALED....32

DAY 8 MAN WITH WITHERED HAND....34

DAY 9 SON OF NOBLEMAN HEALED....36

DAY 10 THE LIVING WATER....39

DAY 11 PRAYER IN GETHSEMANE....42

DAY 12 SLEEP ON NOW, AND TAKE REST....45

DAY 13 DEAD SON OF WIDOW RAISED....................................47

DAY 14 MIRACLE AT BETHESDA POOL.....................................51

DAY 15 THE HEAD CORNER STONE..54

DAY 16 HIS PRECIOUS BLOOD..56

DAY 17 THE LAMB THAT WAS SLAIN..58

DAY 18 JUDAS ISCARIOT BETRAYS..60

DAY 19 THE TRIAL OF JESUS..63

DAY 20 ROLE OF SATAN AT THE CROSS..................................66

DAY 21 PURPOSES OF GOD PREVAIL..69

DAY 22 BLIND FROM BIRTH HEALED..72

DAY 23 TESTIMONY OF THE BLIND MAN..................................75

DAY 24 THE FATHER AND THE SON..78

DAY 25 GLIMSPE OF RESURRECTION......................................81

DAY 26 DISPUTE WITH PHARISEES..85

DAY 27 BLIND SEE..87

DAY 28 DEATH OR SLEEP..90

DAY 29 MARTHA BELIEVED..93

DAY 30 THE FELLOWSHIP..96

OCTOBER DEVOTIONALS 100

DAY 1 MAN AT HIS BEST IS VANITY..101

DAY 2 THE BLESSED HOPE..103

DAY 3 CAN GOD BE CONFINED TO A CERTAIN PLACE?............105

DAY 4 GOD WILL NOT LEAVE US IN LOW PROFILE...................108

DAY 5 THE FEAST OF TRUMPETS..111

DAY 6 LAW AND GRACE 114

DAY 7 PAUL ADMONISHES GALATIANS...................................117

DAY 8 PAUL BLESSES 120

DAY 9 PAUL WARNS GENTILES..123

DAY 10 SIN CAN NOT HAVE DOMINION 126

DAY 11 ANOTHER GOSPEL 129

DAY 12 THE MESSAGE OF CROSS 131

DAY 13 WHO WE WERE? 134

DAY 14 GOD KNOWS OUR WEAKNESS 137

DAY 15 CAN MAN BE SAVED BY OWN EFFORTS 141

DAY 16 REDEMPTION AND JUSTIFICATION............................143

DAY 17 NO MAN SAW GOD 148

DAY 18 OUR BLESSINGS IN ABRAHAM 155

DAY 19 THE EMBLEMS 158

DAY 20 DAVID'S GRATITUDE 161

DAY 21 SUBMIT TO THE WILL OF THE LORD 164

DAY 22 THE SONG OF MOSES 167

DAY 23 SCARLET ROBE AND REED 170

DAY 24 HEZEKIAH DEFEATS SENNACHERIB 174

DAY 25 LEPER HEALED 177

DAY 26 FAITH SAVES (Centurion's Servant healed) 180

DAY 27 PETER'S MOTHER-IN-LAW HEALED 183

DAY 28 DO NOT BE AFRAID 186

DAY 29 IT IS FINISHED 189

DAY 30 THE TRUTH SHALL SET YOU FREE 191

DAY 31 GREAT COMMISSION 194

PREFACE

My mission is to proclaim the good news of our Lord Jesus Christ as revealed to me through Holy Bible and from various teachers, preachers, and commentators. This is my voluntary service to God in the name of His only begotten Son Lord Jesus Christ.

I share the truth of knowledge of God with others with good intention of bringing them to the knowledge of the living God, the God of Abraham, the God of Isaac, the God of Jacob, and the Father of our Lord Jesus Christ. My mission is to proclaim the Gospel of Lord Jesus Christ and not converting forcibly anyone to Christianity.

There are fundamental Christian doctrines that I believe in and I will not compromise on those doctrines. They are:

God is Triune: The Father, The Son and The Holy Spirit. They are not three Gods, but One God in three persons, co-equal-co-existent and functionally different.

There is no salvation except by Grace through Faith in Lord Jesus Christ. I believe in:

"That if thou shalt confess with thy mouth the Lord Jesus, and shalt believe in thine heart that God hath raised him from the dead, thou shalt be saved" (Romans 10:9)

One may accept or reject any or part of my writings/teachings. No offense is meant to any individual or any religion or any organization. Please visit http://www.lesliejohn.net/

I pray for the peace of Jerusalem and desire that all Jews may accept Lord Jesus as their personal Savior and Messiah.

"Pray for the peace of Jerusalem: they shall prosper that love thee" (Psalms 122:6)

I firmly believe in the saying of Jesus, who said:

"No man can come to me, except the Father which hath sent me draw him: and I will raise him up at the last day" John 6:44.

My efforts to teach or preach are of no use unless Lord Jesus Christ Himself intervenes and the Father draws a person unto Him.

All Scriptures in electronic format are from King James Version (KJV) from Open domain, and

English Standard Version (ESV)

Description:

God said to Joshua not to fear but meditate on the word of God day and night; “for then thou shalt make thy way prosperous”.

This book of the law shall not depart out of thy mouth; but thou shalt meditate therein day and night, that thou mayest observe to do according to all that is written therein: for then thou shalt make thy way prosperous, and then thou shalt have good success. Have not I commanded thee? Be strong and of a good courage; be not afraid, neither be thou dismayed: for the LORD thy God is with thee whithersoever thou goest. (Joshua 1:8-9)

This book has 61 Devotionals to facilitate reader to meditate at least one devotional a day.

"I and my Father are one" (John 10:30)

?

SEPTEMBER DEVOTIONALS

DAY 1 STORMS CALMED DOWN

"But the men marvelled, saying, What manner of man is this, that even the winds and the sea obey him!" (Matthew 8:27)

There was great multitude of people following Jesus as they saw the miracles done by Him. They saw how a leper was healed; they saw how centurion's servant was healed and they also saw Peter's mother-in-law was healed.

When Jesus touched Peter's mother-in-law, who was suffering from fever, He was not trying to diagnose her disease, nor was He trying to console her but His touching was a powerful healing-touch that healed her fully.

There was no trace of fatigue left in her nor was she feeling tired anymore but she rose up and ministered unto them.

Jesus looked at the crowd that expected more miracles from Him and said to them to go to the other side of the sea, which was "Sea of Galilee".

Just before leaving to the other side of the sea He had conversation with a scribe who expressed his desire to follow Him but Jesus showed him how hard it was to follow Him.

When Jesus spoke to another he expressed his difficulty in following Him but Jesus said to him to follow Him. He said that those who are spiritually dead may go and attend to their earthly needs. Thus two different types of men were introduced to us; one that half-heartedly expressing his desire to follow Jesus and another with full of excuses when the Lord asked him to follow.

As Jesus entered the ship to go to the other side His disciples followed Him. His sailing by the sea helped future generations to have hope in the Lord that He helps those that seek His help.

Jesus chose to go by sea-way instead of going by the road-way in order that His journey by the sea would be of much comfort to those who usually undertake travel by sea. It was going to be a sure sign for future sailors that they can pray to Him for their safe journey and seek His help.

Jesus was taking rest just as any human would do after tiresome job. Jesus, the Son of God, taking rest shows us that He was fully human when He was in this world.

He was tired and was sleeping but He was not as deep in His sleep as Jonah was, many years ago, in the ship while trying to escape to a possible secure place from the task he was assigned. In Jesus we have our salvation. He is our redeemer.

As they were journeying there arose a vigorous tempest in the sea so much that the waves from the sea covered the ship. Indeed, everyone in the ship, except Jesus, was afraid of the tempest. Their nerves started shrinking as they saw the tempest even when the creator of the seas was right there in their midst.

How often we also fear, in spite of having faith in Jesus, that some misadventure would overtake us. The Lord would have to remind us through some servant of God or through His word that He is always there with us. Indeed, He is our comfort and sustainer. It is worth recollecting Psalmist's comforting words.

"O love the LORD, all ye his saints: for the LORD preserveth the faithful, and plentifully rewardeth the proud doer. Be of good courage, and he shall strengthen your heart, all ye that hope in the LORD" (Psalms 31:23-24)

Jesus could have ordered the sea to be calm even before they started their journey or when they were sailing but He preferred not to do so and He showed that He was in control of the situation, over waters and the storms that His disciples may become stronger in their faith in Him.

When the severity of the storm increased the disciples were afraid. The disciples went to Lord Jesus, who was sleeping in the same ship, and awoke Him. They begged saying "Lord, save us: we perish". T

hey were praying for not only themselves but on behalf of all the sailors. They thought the storms would drown the ship. However, they realized that the Lord of the sea was in ship, and He would be able to save them. Therefore, they prayed to Jesus to save them and Jesus heard their prayer.

Jesus admonished them that they are fearful because they lacked faith. Then He arose and rebuked the winds and sea and there was great calm. The men in the ship marveled at the miracle and wondered about the power that Jesus exercised on storms and on the winds that they obeyed His command.

Indeed Lord Jesus Christ was the Savior. Much more than the comfort that we have that our Lord has the power over storms we cast our burden on Him and rest in His arms because He gave us salvation free of cost.

While those whose sins are not forgiven and do not have Lord Jesus Christ as their savior would have to gnash their teeth in the "Lake of fire", where fire never quenches, we will be with Him for ever and ever.

"And he saith unto them, Why are ye fearful, O ye of little faith? Then he arose, and rebuked the winds and the sea; and there was a great calm" (Matthew 8:26)

Sample Prayer: O LORD my God, all glory is unto you and you alone. You are Almighty God, you calmed down storms. I believe you will calm down storms that cause confusion and disturbance in my life. Please take charge of me and my mind and my emotions. I pray In Lord Jesus Christ's name, Amen.

(Please introduce in your prayer daily the corresponding content)

DAY 2 JESUS CASTS OUT DEVILS

Lord Jesus, the Son of God, had power to subdue not only diseases namely leprosy, fever etc. and over the storms but He also had power over demons. (Ref. Matthew 8:28-34)

Jesus was in the country of Gergesenes and He saw two possessed with devils that were coming out from the tombs. The residence of these demons was among the dead in the tombs and they were so fierce that no man could pass by that way. Devils love to be among, and in the hearts of, the dead spiritually.

When the devils saw Jesus, who was the Son of God, they realized His divinity and cried out as to why He was out there where they reside because they had nothing in common with Him. They belonged to the kingdom of devils and Jesus was from the kingdom of God.

It was evident from the incident as we read in Matthew Chapter 12:24-30 where Pharisees accused Jesus that he cast out devils with the help of Beelzebub, the prince of devils. The devils are united when they fight against the children of God and they do not divide among themselves to split their kingdom.

Jesus perceived their thoughts and said to them that every kingdom divided against itself will end up in destruction of its own kingdom similar to that of a house that is divided itself would not stand. He then questioned Pharisees if Satan casts out Satan how would his kingdom stand. If that was so, the kingdom of Satan would, then, be divided. Jesus proceeds further by giving answer that if He casts out devils from them by the Spirit of God; surely the kingdom of God comes into them.

Satan and his angels have nothing to do with the incarnate God, Lord Jesus Christ, who relinquished His glory in heaven and came down to earth in the form of servant and in the likeness of men. Lord Jesus Christ and God the Father are one, as He himself stated.

The devils feared that Jesus was there to torment them before their due time. Obviously, the devils had their own time given out by God Himself, and, therefore, the devils asked Him as to why He was there and questioned Him if He was there to torment them before their time lapsed. It is worth recollecting Job's story here.

When Satan was in the presence of God and the 'sons of God' came before God Satan also came along them to Him. It was God who started the conversation first and He said to Satan as to whether he saw a righteous man, Job. Then, Satan sought permission to afflict Job and then see if Job still remained without cursing God.

On hearing this challenge God gave permission to Satan with limited power over Job that he may afflict but not touch his soul. From this it is evident that Satan has no power over the child of God to test or afflict over and above the limits permitted by God. Satan cannot over step the limits that God prescribes.

It was a similar situation here and, therefore, the devils asked the Son of God as to why He was there before it was their due time. The devils besought Lord Jesus to allow them to enter swine by the sea side. Jesus permitted them to enter swine which, thereafter, ran violently into the sea and perished.

DAY 3 ALMIGHTY GOD AND HIS POWER

The keepers of the swine learnt that Jesus cast out devils from two men and the devils were allowed to enter into swine which ran violently into sea and perished.

Then, they requested Him to leave their city. In spite of the fact that Jesus did miracle to deliver the men from the devils the people preferred that the deliverer should leave their city.

It can be observed that even in our present day similar situations prevail where people prefer to live in sin and entertain Satan that brings temptations and torments excluding God from among them.

Inasmuch as the chief angel of the angels, the creation of God, rebelled against God and became Satan, the adversary, the Satan is somewhat equal but not fully so in status to that of the mighty angel Michael and far below in status and power to that of God.

This is evident from the fact that Michael fought once with the devil successfully to take the body of Moses, and next successfully fought and delivered the messenger who was held by the dragon for twenty one days before he went and revealed prophecy to Daniel.

Yet another time John saw in his vision that there was a great war between Michael and his angels who fought Satan down to defeat and his place was not found any more in heaven.

Jude bore record that even when Michael the archangel was contending with the devil and disputed about the body of Moses he did not bring railing accusation; but rather said "The Lord rebuke thee". God hid the burial place of Moses and no one knew until this day where he was buried. God Himself took care of the burial of his servant Moses. The evidence that Moses appeared along with Elijah during the transfiguration of Jesus indicates that Moses was raised despite fierce opposition from Satan.

"So Moses the servant of the LORD died there in the land of Moab, according to the word of the LORD. And he buried him in a valley in the land of Moab, over against Bethpeor: but no man knoweth of his sepulchre unto this day" (Deuteronomy 34:5-6)

"Yet Michael the archangel, when contending with the devil he disputed about the body of Moses, durst not bring against him a railing accusation, but said, The Lord rebuke thee" (Jude 1:9)

When Daniel fasted to know the truth about the end days a messenger came to him and said that when he was on his way to reveal the prophecy to him Satan who was in the prince of the kingdom of Persia withstood him for twenty one days; but Michael the archangel helped him and that is how he was there to reveal how the last days would be.

"But the prince of the kingdom of Persia withstood me one and twenty days: but, lo, Michael, one of the chief princes, came to help me; and I remained there with the kings of Persia. Now I am come to make thee understand what shall befall thy people in the latter days: for yet the vision is for many days" (Daniel 10:13-14)

"And there was war in heaven: Michael and his angels fought against the dragon; and the dragon fought and his angels, And prevailed not; neither was their place found any more in heaven" (Revelation 12:7-8)

There are few facts that we can learn from the dispossession of the devils from the two men by Lord Jesus Christ. First of all, this is strong evidence by the fact that Jews abhorred swine in general, that Gentiles also lived in Israel during the period when Jesus was on this earth.

Secondly, the devils knew their destiny on this earth and also their destiny in the "Lake of fire" after "great white throne" judgment (cf. Rev 20:11).

Thirdly, Jesus wanted to teach the people that the devils do harm men just as they did to the swine and, therefore, He allowed the swine to be destroyed instead of men in whom they resided. Lord Jesus was and is the only deliverer from such torment and sin.

Fourthly, it was in the Almighty God's power to take away the possession of the owners of the swine and destroy their possession. (Ref. Matthew 8:28-34)

DAY 4 DAY OF ATONEMENT

"Also on the tenth day of this seventh month there shall be a day of atonement: it shall be an holy convocation unto you; and ye shall afflict your souls, and offer an offering made by fire unto the LORD" (Leviticus 23:27).

The "Day of Atonement" was celebrated by Israelites on the tenth day of seventh month as a memorial of the way the High Priest went into the "Holy of Holies" and sprinkled of the blood of the goat on which the lottery fell as "for the Lord" (Leviticus 16:8-9) and also as memorial of the second goat which was the "Scapegoat". The two goats collectively were the shadow of the sacrifice of Jesus on the cross and bearing the sins of the sinner.

"And Aaron shall cast lots upon the two goats; one lot for the LORD, and the other lot for the scapegoat" (Leviticus 16:8).

This is the sixth feast of the seven feasts described in Leviticus Chapter 23.

The great Day of Atonement was the shadow of the crucifixion of Lord Jesus Christ who died on behalf of us bearing our sin outside the gates of the city.

Gospel writers Matthew, Mark, and John used the word "Golgotha", which means "place of skulls". Luke used the word "Calvary" instead of "Golgotha" and Calvary means "Cranium" which again means the same as "skull".

(Matthew 27:33, Mark 15:22, Luke 23:33, John 19:17)

"For he hath made him to be sin for us, who knew no sin; that we might be made the righteousness of God in him" 2 Corinthians 5:21.

The sacrifices offered in the Old Testament period covered their sins, but they were not forgiven forever. They had to do it again the next year.

In the New Testament period we are privileged that we do not need to offer such sacrifices repeatedly. Christ died for our sake once and for all; and that was enough. Our part is to believe Jesus as our Savior and repent of our sins to him. Jesus is the mediator for us and He is our High priest.

"But Christ being come an high priest of good things to come, by a greater and more perfect tabernacle, not made with hands, that is to say, not of this building; Neither by the blood of goats and calves, but by his own blood he entered in once into the holy place, having obtained eternal redemption for us" (Hebrews 9:11-12)

"So Christ was once offered to bear the sins of many; and unto them that look for him shall he appear the second time without sin unto salvation". (Hebrews 9:28)

The blood of Jesus Christ cleansed the sins of the Old Testament Saints, and also the New Testament saints. Lord Jesus became the High Priest, after the order of Melchisedec, thus setting aside the imperfect sacrificial offerings of the Old Testament. Jesus was the Savior in the past, He is the Savior now, and He will be the Savior in future. Hebrews Chapters 9, 10 and 11 detail the way Jesus became perfect sacrifice for all.

DAY 5 STRIVING WITH MAN

"And the LORD said, My spirit shall not always strive with man, for that he also is flesh: yet his days shall be an hundred and twenty years" (Genesis 6:3)

In the days of Noah the wickedness on this earth increased so much that God saw it and said in His heart that every imagination of the thoughts of man is evil continually and He felt sorry for having created man. God could not tolerate such sin as that prevailed during those days and punished mankind with floods.

It rained for forty days and forty nights and every living creature except eight souls of the family of Noah and the selected number of animals, birds and creeping things were saved.

As the mankind increased after Noah's period God saw that mankind sinned against Him beyond His tolerance limits and He destroyed mankind in Sodom and Gomorrah with fire and brimstone and none except Lot was saved.

God scattered the "House of Israel" for committing sin against Him. They worshipped Baal and Ashtaroth and burnt incense to them resulting in invasion of their kingdom by Assyrians who took them captive because God's anger was kindled against them.

Solomon went after many wives, concubines and worshipped their gods and the God of Israel rent his kingdom into two resulting in Babylonians taking captive of the "House of Judah".

Man never ceased from committing sin and God always contended with the spirit of man. Prophets came and warned mankind about the destructions that would come about but men killed them.

God sent His one and only Son, Lord Jesus Christ, to save man but men killed Him as well. However, Lord Jesus, was raised from the dead and now He is alive and seated on the right hand of the Majesty. God forgives any sin except blaspheme of the Holy Spirit.

It is as simple as confessing that Jesus is the Lord and confess sins by mouth to Him and believe in heart that God raised Jesus from the dead. But if man keeps resisting the call from God and intentionally falls into sin time and again then God hands him over to his sinful life.

"Now the just shall live by faith: but if any man draw back, my soul shall have no pleasure in him" (Hebrews 10:38)

In the history of mankind it can be seen that whenever man committed sin, and caused anger in the heart of God, man was either punished severely or was chastised so that he may come back to Him again.

However there is comfort in the words of Psalmist who said God is compassionate and longsuffering and plenteous in mercy. God will not reject anyone who confesses his/her sins to Him and accept Jesus as their Lord.

But thou, O Lord, art a God full of compassion, and gracious, longsuffering, and plenteous in mercy and truth. (Psalms 86:15)

The LORD set a bow in the sky after the floods during Noah's period and said He will remember His covenant and shall not destroy all the mankind on the earth anymore by floods. (Ref. Genesis 6:5, 6, Genesis 19:14-15)

"And I will remember my covenant, which is between me and you and every living creature of all flesh; and the waters shall no more become a flood to destroy all flesh" (Genesis 9:15)

DAY 6 SIN AMONG ROMANS

Apostle Paul was a very powerful servant of God and he preached repentance and to accept Jesus as the Lord. He was the chosen servant of God, exalting the name of the One and Only God. He expressed his grief on the behavior of those, who did not glorify God and because they were not thankful to God.

They rather consistently harbored wild imaginations resulting in their perception being darkened.

During the period when Paul preached among Romans he observed that they chose to become fools by exalting themselves as wise by making the incorruptible and mighty God into an idol that appeared either as a bird, beast, or creeping thing.

Therefore, God gave them up to their own desires of lusts and uncleanness that took root in their hearts. They preferred to dishonor their bodies among themselves men giving up to the vile desires unto their fellow men, and women giving up to the vile desires unto their fellow women through the unnatural use of the body that is against the nature.

Some of them not only committed those sins that were detestable but took pleasure in committing them despite their knowledge that such sin brings death (Ref. Romans 1:22-32)

They burned with passion one for another of the same gender working among themselves against the way God has chosen it to be, resulting in grave error and debasement of their proclaimed knowledge.

They longed to enhance their desires of "unrighteousness, fornication, wickedness, covetousness, maliciousness. They were full of envy and were whisperers, backbiters, haters of God, despiteful, proud, boasters, inventors of evil things, disobedient to parents and covenant-breakers".

Therefore, God gave them up to their own desires of lusts and uncleanness. This is the reason why Paul says that he was not ashamed to proclaim the gospel of Christ. The gospel is power unto salvation for those who believe in it and foolishness for those who do not believe in it.

"For the wrath of God is revealed from heaven against all ungodliness and unrighteousness of men, who hold the truth in unrighteousness" (Romans 1:18)

Exercising faith in Jesus helps us to grow in Him leaping from one step to another and building up oneself strong enough to face the attacks from the enemy. Troubles might come and God might chasten; yet it gives the child of God opportunity to grow continually in Him.

There is every opportunity to fall away from the truth of the knowledge of the living God because Satan is very cunning and ever-active to misguide and mislead not only those who do not believe in Jesus but also those who believe in Him. Satan is very active among the believers rather than the unbelievers. Sometimes Satan comes as a roaring lion and sometimes like one that is transformed into an angel of light.

"And no marvel; for Satan himself is transformed into an angel of light" (2 Corinthians 11:14)

Are you resisting the will and call of God continually? If so, God might hand you over to the wiles of the devil and to your sinful desires; but if you repent of your sins and accept Lord Jesus Christ as your personal Savior there is everlasting life waiting for you.

Our bodies are temples of God and Spirit of God dwells in us. If anyone defiles the temple of God it is tantamount to involving God in our defilement of the body. God never takes part in our falling but rather He helps us with chastisement to recover from the falling away from the truth.

If still we follow our own ways then God would hand over us to the wiles of our evil desires and allow us to reap the consequences in the body, perhaps in the form of serious diseases. Salvation is secure unless one goes to the extent of trampling the blood of Lord Jesus Christ under his/her foot. (cf. 1 Corinthians 3:16-17, 1 Corinthians 6:19, 2 Corinthians 6:16, Hebrews 10:26)

However, those who are saved by the blood of Lord Jesus Christ will always be in His fold never venturing to commit sins. His blood cleanses us from all unrighteousness.

The Lord says:

"My Father, which gave them me, is greater than all; and no man is able to pluck them out of my Father's hand" (John 10:29)

DAY 7 PARALYTIC HEALED

Although Jesus did miracles and healed many His primary purpose was to preach repentance and to let them know that the "Kingdom of heaven" was at hand. Yet, people who came to Him did come with much hope that He would heal the sick and cast away unclean spirits from the afflicted people.

There was one sick with palsy who was helped by his four friends. They brought him on a bed to the home where Jesus was preaching.

There was so much crowd in the home that there was no way for the four friends, of the man that suffered from palsy, to enter into the house and place the sick man before Jesus. Undaunted, they took the patient straight onto the roof-top of the house, removed a part of the roof, and let the patient down from the roof and placed right before Jesus.

There were scribes who watched if Jesus healed the palsy on Sabbath day. Jesus was pleased with the faith the four friends, who placed the man with palsy for healing.

Jesus questioned if it was right to do good or bad on the Sabbath day and then said to the man suffering with palsy "Son, thy sins be forgiven thee". Scribes and Pharisees reasoned vigorously as to who Jesus was to say "Son, thy sins be forgiven thee". They considered it as blaspheme because they all knew that only God can forgive sins. They reasoned so because they were ignorant of the truth about Jesus Christ. Jesus was the son of God, very God Himself.

Lord Jesus perceived their thoughts and questioned them if it was easier for Him to forgive sins or to say to the palsy to rise up, take his bed and walk. He emphasized on the point that He had the power to forgive sins and He did exactly that. He granted the man forgiveness from his sins and then He said to the man sick with palsy to rise up, take up his bed and walk.

"Giving thanks unto the Father, which hath made us meet to be partakers of the inheritance of the saints in light: Who hath delivered us from the power of darkness, and hath translated us into the kingdom of his dear Son:

In whom we have redemption through his blood, even the forgiveness of sins: Who is the image of the invisible God, the firstborn of every creature" (Colossians 1:12-15)

"If we say that we have no sin, we deceive ourselves, and the truth is not in us. If we confess our sins, he is faithful and just to forgive us [our] sins, and to cleanse us from all unrighteousness. If we say that we have not sinned, we make him a liar, and his word is not in us" 1 John 1:8-10

DAY 8 MAN WITH WITHERED HAND

The existence of Law in any society invites a class of scholars who devote assiduously to the Law. In the Bible also there is mention of such scribes.

On a Sabbath day while Jesus was teaching in synagogue He saw a man, whose right hand was withered, in the audience.

Pharisees and scribes watched very closely to see if Jesus healed the man with withered hand and find an accusation against Him. According to Mosaic Law violation of Sabbath invited stoning by death.

"Ye shall keep the sabbath therefore; for it is holy unto you: every one that defileth it shall surely be put to death: for whosoever doeth any work therein, that soul shall be cut off from among his people". (Exodus 31:14)

According to New Testament and Flavius Joseph, Jewish historian the major sects of Jews were (1) Pharisees, (2) Sadducees and (3) Essenes.

Pharisees were wealthy who separated from common people. They were proud, haughty, self-righteous, and held common people in disrespect (Ref. John 7:49). The words of Jesus stirred up contentions among them and Pharisees tried to play down the teachings of Jesus.

Lord Jesus knew the thoughts of scribes and Pharisees, and said to the man, who was suffering from withered hand, to rise up and stand forth in their midst.

The man stood forth. Then, Jesus asked them if it was lawful to do good on the Sabbath day or to do evil and to save life or to destroy it. He then, said to the man to stretch forth his hand and he did. The man's withered hand was restored whole as the other hand. The scribes and Pharisees were angry on Him and went away. Jesus said on the last day of "feast of tabernacles"

"...if any man thirst, let him come unto me, and drink. He that believeth on me, as the scripture hath said, out of his belly shall flow rivers of living water. (But this spake he of the Spirit, which they that believe on him should receive: for the Holy Ghost was not yet given; because that Jesus was not yet glorified.)" (John 7:37-39)

DAY 9 SON OF NOBLEMAN HEALED

Jesus went to Cana second time where He performed His first miracle by turning water into wine at a wedding. During his second visit to Cana he saw a nobleman coming to him with a fervent request that Jesus should visit his home at Capernaum to heal his son, who was on death bed. The narration of this healing is recorded only in John's Gospel.

The Gospel writers did not identify the sequence of miracles and healings performed by Jesus, and, therefore, it is hard to identify which miracle and healing were the first ones to be performed by Him.

However, the miraculous turning of water into wine at Cana is thought to be the first miracle and the healing of Nobleman's son was thought to the first one. Or, this healing could be one among the others recorded in Matthew 4:23; thus making a point that sequence is not as important as the gist of the message conveyed through the miracles and healings.

"And Jesus went about all Galilee, teaching in their synagogues, and preaching the gospel of the kingdom, and healing all manner of sickness and all manner of disease among the people" (Matthew 4:23)

Nobleman wished to see signs and wonders in order to believe in Jesus just as others wished to see. Jesus said to him "...Except ye see signs and wonders, ye will not believe" John 4:48

The nobleman insisted without ceasing that Jesus may visit his home and heal his son. Perhaps, he thought the only way to have his son healed was by inviting Jesus into His house and presenting the patient physically before Him in order that Jesus may perform miraculous healing; but Jesus spoke and immediately nobleman's son was healed.

Jesus showed to the nobleman, as also to others, that His word was enough to heal his son. Jesus said to him "Go thy way; thy son liveth". The nobleman believed that his son would be healed and went his way. On his way home his servants met him and told him that his son was healed and he lives.

The nobleman was curious to know the hour of his son's healing and they said "Yesterday at the seventh hour the fever left him". The nobleman knew that it was the same hour when Jesus said to him "Go thy way; thy son liveth". This miraculous healing of nobleman's son helped him and his family to believe in Jesus. (Ref. John 4:43-54)

This reminds us the words of Jesus in Matthew 4:4 and also another healing he performed on Centurion's servant.

"But he answered and said, It is written, Man shall not live by bread alone, but by every word that proceedeth out of the mouth of God" (Matthew 4:4)

"And Jesus said unto the centurion, Go thy way; and as

thou hast believed, so be it done unto thee. And his servant was healed in the selfsame hour" (Matthew 8:13)

How often we forget that God spoke everything in heaven, earth and in the seas into existence by His word. Believe in Jesus and receive salvation free of cost. Salvation cannot be bought with silver or gold or good works; it is received by faith in Jesus Christ and that God raised Him from the dead.

"Verily, verily, I say unto you, He that heareth my word, and believeth on him that sent me, hath everlasting life, and shall not come into condemnation; but is passed from death unto life" (John 5:24)

DAY 10 THE LIVING WATER

Once when Lord Jesus Christ was in the city of Samaria certain woman from that city went to Jacob's well to fetch water. On seeing the woman fetching water Jesus asked her water to drink; but then the woman recognized that He was a Jew. She asked Him as to why He was asking water from her because Jews had no dealings with the Gentiles.

It is worth noting here that the Gentiles are those who are not the descendants of Jacob. Samaritans are mixed generation, the offspring from Jacob's descendants, and the Gentiles. They are those who were not proselytized to be equated with the Israelites. That is the reason why Samaritan woman could say 'our fathers' referring to Jacob and his descendants but she was not Israelite.

Samaria was inhabited by the people brought into that city by the Assyrians, from the cities that they captured in war, while fighting with kings of northern kingdom of Israel.

The people thus brought into Samaria settled down there, as replacement of the people, of the "House of Israel" carried away as captives by the Assyrians. The scattering of the "House of Israel" was in consequence of God's anger against them, because they worshipped Baal and Ashteroth, the goddesses of nations. Worshipping these goddesses was encouraged by Jezebel, the wicked wife of King Ahab.

Jesus said to the Samaritan woman that if she knew who she was speaking to, and if she asked for water from Him, He would have given the living water. She wondered as to how He could have given her the living water, because he had nothing to fetch water from that well, which was very deep. Further, she asked if He was greater than Jacob, who gave them the well, from which he, and his children, and his cattle drank water.

The Samaritan woman did not understand the point that Jesus was making. While Jesus was showing her the way to the "Kingdom of God", she was thinking of earthly things. Jesus was speaking of heavenly blessings; but she was thinking of earthly blessings.

Jesus said to her that whoever drank water from the well would thirst again, but if anyone drank the living water that He gave, he will never thirst again. He said that the living water in him will spring up into everlasting life.

Again the woman perceived the talk from Jesus as for earthly blessings, and craved for that living water, that He would give, in order that she may not thirst again, and cease from fetching water from the well.

The conversation continued and Jesus having known her heart, and her life as well, said to her to go and bring her husband. The woman replied that she had five husbands in the past, but presently she had no husband; moreover the one whom with she was living was not her husband. Jesus appreciated her truthful confession.

After He spoke to the woman, about the living water that He would give her, if she believed in Him, she left her water pot at the well, and went to the city, and testified about Jesus, the Savior. Her testimony yielded much result when many Samaritans of that city believed on Him. They besought Jesus to stay with them and He abode there for two days and many more believed in Him.

"And many more believed because of his own word; And said unto the woman, Now we believe, not because of thy saying: for we have heard him ourselves, and know that this is indeed the Christ, the Saviour of the world" (John 4:41-42)

Lord Jesus Christ gives everlasting life to those who believe in Him. This is the time to repent and confess your sins to Him, and believe that Jesus bore your sins on Himself, and died on the cross; He was buried and was raised from the dead.

"But whosoever drinketh of the water that I shall give him shall never thirst; but the water that I shall give him shall be in him a well of water springing up into everlasting life" (John 4:14)

DAY 11 PRAYER IN GETHSEMANE

"And he went a little further, and fell on his face, and prayed, saying, O my Father, if it be possible, let this cup pass from me: nevertheless not as I will, but as thou wilt" (Matthew 26:39)

Just before Jesus was arrested He went to a place called "Gethsemane" in the Mount of Olives along with His disciples. He took three disciples, namely, Peter, James and John, who were very close to Him, to pray.

He was very sorrowful about the impending death, wherein He had to bear the sin of the world, and lay His life for our sake. His sorrow was not because He was going to be arrested, or face a trial, which of course, proved to be an illegal one, but because the sin of mankind that He was going to bear was very heavy.

"When Jesus had spoken these words, he went forth with his disciples over the brook Cedron, where was a garden, into the which he entered, and his disciples". (John 18:1)

It pleased the Father to bruise Him and pay the penalty for our sake and the very purpose of Jesus coming into this world, was to lay His life for our sake, taking upon Him, the curse of man and redeem us from perishing (cf. Isaiah 53:10). His love for us was so great that He relinquished His glory in heaven, emptied Himself, and came in the form of servant, and in the likeness of man. It is so amazing that God, who was so un-approachable during the Old Testament period, humbled Himself so much so that He became man for our sake, and was in this world. He was fully divine and fully man on this earth.

"In the beginning was the Word, and the Word was with God, and the Word was God". (John 1:1)"And the Word was made flesh, and dwelt among us, (and we beheld his glory, the glory as of the only begotten of the Father,) full of grace and truth" (John 1:14)

Jesus taught repentance and said the "kingdom of heaven" was at hand. He was born Jew and was their Messiah; yet they did not understand the truth. He healed sick, cast away evil spirits from those who were afflicted by them.

While He was in the Garden of Gethsemane, He said to His disciples to pray, and went little farther and fell on His face and prayed to the Father saying, "O my Father, if it be possible, let this cup pass from me: nevertheless not as I will, but as thou wilt".

Notice Jesus prayed to the Father that if it were possible the death that He was going to face may pass; yet He said everything may be done, not according to His will, but according the will of the Father.

If He prayed that the cup may pass without laying any condition, the Father would have, perhaps, agreed, and the purpose for which He came into this world would have been defeated.

It was not the purpose of Jesus either to set aside that cup of suffering, but because He saw that the sin of mankind was so grave that He thought, for a while, it may pass away from Him; yet very quickly He added to His prayer the words "nevertheless not as I will, but as thou wilt".

Jesus surrendered Himself to the will of the Father and prayed with much intense that being in agony His "sweat was as it were great drops of blood falling down to the ground".

DAY 12 SLEEP ON NOW, AND TAKE REST

"And being in an agony he prayed more earnestly: and his sweat was as it were great drops of blood falling down to the ground". (Luke 22:44).

Jesus, after praying, in the Garden of Gethsemane, went back to the disciples, and saw that they were sleeping and He said to Peter, "sleepest thou? couldest not thou watch one hour? Watch ye and pray, lest ye enter into temptation".

How often, we also sleep when God gives us great responsibility! Jesus admonished them to pray that they may not enter into temptation. True, prayer keeps us away from temptations.

Prayer brings relief to our problems, trials, and temptations. God knows that we are made out of dust and, that is the reason, why He forgives us. His disciples were so dear to Him, and therefore, He consoled them saying "The spirit truly is ready, but the flesh is weak".

Jesus went again and repeated the same prayer because bearing of sin of man was so heavy on Him and He returned to see His disciples sleeping again.

They were not in a mood to answer Jesus because their eyes were so heavy. Jesus went the third time to the same place, where He went twice before, and repeated the same prayer. He came back and saw His disciples were sleeping again. He said to them "Sleep on now, and take your rest: it is enough, the hour is come; behold, the Son of man is betrayed into the hands of sinners".

How sad it is that we sleep when God gives us some responsibility and then we may have to hear from Him "Sleep on now, and take your rest". When Elijah said to the LORD that He was the only one to serve Him, God said to Him that He reserved seven thousand who did not bow their heads to Baal. God's work will never stop if we withdraw from serving Him.

Jesus suffered for our sake on the cross. After His death, He was buried and His body did not see corruption. He was triumphant over death, and rose from the dead on the third day. He appeared to many during His for forty days' time, that He was on this earth, before ascending into Heaven. He is seated on the right hand of the Majesty and pleading on our behalf. He will come again soon to judge the quick and the dead.

Please accept Jesus as your personal Savior and receive everlasting life.

DAY 13 DEAD SON OF WIDOW RAISED

In what seems to be a small passage in the book of Luke 7th chapter verses from 11-17, we have glimpse of life after death, the resurrection. We have the hope that we are not going to be non-existent after death, but that we will live after death to be with our Lord for ever and ever.

Jesus had been compassionate to all those who sought His intervention in their lives seeking either healing or the truth about the 'Kingdom of God'.

It is a small city where Jesus performed this miracle of raising the dead to life. He was going with His disciples into a small city called "Nain", where He saw a dead boy. The dead body of widow's son was being carried out of the city in an open coffin. As He was passing by He saw this dead body and knew that the boy was the only son, the only sustenance of the widow.

There was a crowd of people in the funeral procession, and there was a crowd of people who followed Jesus to witness His miracles and to listen to His teaching. He taught the words of wisdom, repentance and life in His kingdom.

When the Lord came near the coffin he saw and had compassion on the widow and said to her "Weep not". In usual circumstances His words "Weep not" would have angered the widow and the people in the funeral procession as well; but He being the Son of God, touched the bier first, and spoke His powerful words. The funeral procession stopped and the widow, perhaps, looked forward for some answer.

Jesus did miracle; that which would seem to others as improbable. He called the dead boy, as if he was alive saying "Young man, I say unto thee, Arise".

This reminds of Paul's quote in Romans 4:17 where he recollects God's promise to Abraham speaking in past tense as if God had already made Him the father of many nations, and in quickening the dead; calling those things which were non-existent as though they were existent (Ref. Genesis 17:5)

"(As it is written, I have made thee a father of many nations,) before him whom he believed, even God, who quickeneth the dead, and calleth those things which be not as though they were". (Romans 4:17)

To the surprise of all onlookers, the dead boy sat up and began to speak, and Jesus gave the live boy to his widow mother. It was all because of Lord Jesus Christ's compassion on the widow, who had only one son, and he was her only refuge. She was left destitute when her son died.

This was, indeed, a very pitiable situation, even in the sight of men. The Lord being compassionate was moved in His heart and voluntarily stepped forward to help the widow.

Even before anyone asked Him to help the widow, or even before the widow prayed for help, He had compassion on her and touched the bier, and then, brought life back into her dead son.

No doubt, seeing such an unusual act, fear came upon all and they glorified God. They proclaimed that which they understood about Jesus, and said, a great prophet rose among them and God visited them. That rumor of Jesus spread forth throughout Judaea, and throughout all the regions. (cf. Luke 7:11-17)

God sent His one and only begotten Son, Lord Jesus Christ, into this world and He did miracles and wonders and healed sick. He cast out unclean spirits from men. He gave a glimpse of life after death.

He showed that death is not cessation of life, but there is life beyond death. Although those whom He raised to life such as the widow's son, the daughter of Jairus, and Lazarus, who died again, in His own death and resurrection He showed that those who believe in Him will have everlasting life.

Jesus took our sin upon Him and gave His life on behalf of us in order that we might have salvation free of cost. Jesus is the way, the truth, and the life and no one can have everlasting life unless his/her sins are washed in His precious blood.

"Forasmuch as ye know that ye were not redeemed with corruptible things, as silver and gold, from your vain conversation received by tradition from your fathers; But with the precious blood of Christ, as of a lamb without blemish and without spot" (1 Peter 1:18-19)

DAY 14 MIRACLE AT BETHESDA POOL

"Afterward Jesus findeth him in the temple, and said unto him, Behold, thou art made whole: sin no more, lest a worse thing come unto thee" (John 5:14)

On the day of feast of the Jews, i.e. the Passover feast, Jesus went up to Jerusalem where at the 'sheep market' also called 'sheep gate', there was a pool which had five porches, and which in Hebrew language was called "Bethesda".

The pool was of great interest because an angel went there at a certain season and troubled the water in the pool. Upon troubling the water, the first sick person, such as impotent, or blind, or limp, or withered, who gets into the water, was made whole of whatever disease he had.

There was a man, suffering from an infirmity, lying at the pool for thirty eight years, and being unable to get into the pool by himself, when the water was troubled, and no one to help him to get into it, continued to suffer, while someone else got into the water before he could. Jesus saw him lay there, and knew that the man was at the pool for many years, and therefore, had compassion on him, and asked him if he wished to be made whole.

The impotent man answered and said to Jesus that even before he attempted to get into the pool, when the angel troubled the water in it, someone else got into it, and was made whole. Then, Jesus said to him to "Rise, take up thy bed, and walk".

It was the Sabbath day when Jesus healed the impotent man, and the Jews saw the man walking with his bed. They said to him that it was the Sabbath day, and it was unlawful for him to carry his bed. Violation of Sabbath invited death by Stoning as per Mosaic Law.

"Ye shall keep the sabbath therefore; for it is holy unto you: every one that defileth it shall surely be put to death: for whosoever doeth any work therein, that soul shall be cut off from among his people". (Exodus 31:14)

However, the man, who was healed of his disease, said to the Jews "He that made me whole, the same said unto me, Take up thy bed, and walk". The Jews insisted on him to identify the man who healed him and asked him to walk with his bed on the Sabbath day; but the man did not know, who He was, because of great multitude and also because Jesus had left the scene after the incident.

Jesus saw the man in the temple and said to him "Behold, thou art made whole: sin no more, lest a worse thing come unto thee." Jesus cautioned the man that if he sinned again worse could come upon him.

The man departed from the temple and told the Jews that it was Jesus, who healed him. Therefore, the Jews followed Jesus to see how they might take hold of him and slay Him because he healed the man and said to him to walk with his bed on the Sabbath day.

What if the man thought of disobeying the command from Jesus to "Rise, take up thy bed, and walk" thinking that he was already there for thirty eight years lying on the bed waiting for miraculous healing? When Jews asked him who that was who healed him, the man could not say who he was! He could identify Jesus only when he saw Him for the second time in the temple.

The answer is that he would have remained impotent forever; but he chose to obey the command from Jesus in faith.

Jesus healed the man who was helpless, and gave what seemed to be an impossible command demanding great faith and obedience. The man was obedient to the command by faith and eventually he rose up and walked with his bed.

Secondly, Jesus gave an additional command that he should not sin again, otherwise, the worse could happen. We have a lesson here that sinning after being healed of sickness could result in worse coming upon us. The man's obedience and faith healed him. (Ref. John 5:1-14)

DAY 15 THE HEAD CORNER STONE

"The stone which the builders refused is become the head stone of the corner" (Psalms 118:22)

Peter and John, the disciples of Jesus Christ, preached the Gospel and the resurrection from the dead. They healed an impotent man in the name of Jesus. Their ministry was blessed and the number of believers increased from three thousand to five thousand.

This kind of preaching, and miracles, in the name of Jesus, grieved the high priest Annas, Caiaphas, and Alexander, who thought that the preaching belonged to them, and there is no resurrection from the dead.

Sadducees did not believe in the resurrection, and as they were against this teaching they laid hands on Peter and John, the disciples of Jesus, for a trial the next day. The elders, scribes, Annas, the high priest and high priest's kindred gathered at Jerusalem and questioned the authority by which they healed the impotent man, and preached the resurrection from the dead.

Peter, then, filled with Holy Spirit, spoke to them and said to them very firmly that they preached and healed the impotent man in the name of Jesus Christ of Nazareth, whom they crucified, and whom God raised from the dead.

Jesus is the stone, who these elders, Pharisees, Sadducees

rejected, but God set him as the Chief corner stone. David prophesied about Jesus, who was the stone, that the builders rejected, yet the LORD made him the head stone of the corner.

"And have ye not read this scripture; The stone which the builders rejected is become the head of the corner" (Mark 12:10)

Peter and John, the disciples of Jesus, who walked with him, witnessed that Jesus was the stone, whom the Jews rejected, but he became the head stone of the corner. They affirm that there is no other name under heaven where anyone can find salvation.

One may object to this preaching but the Bible says it very firmly that there is no salvation except by believing that Jesus is the Savior. Peter and John, the Apostles, who were not learned, or educated, boldly said these things because they were with Jesus and took knowledge from him, who is the only begotten Son of God. The accusers attempted to execute the disciples of Jesus but did not find any cause to punish them, and let them go.

"Unto you therefore which believe he is precious: but unto them which be disobedient, the stone which the builders disallowed, the same is made the head of the corner" (1 Peter 2:7) [Cf. Acts 4:1-14, Ps 118:21-23. Isa. 28:16, Ro 9:33, Eph. 2:20, 1Pe 2:7]

DAY 16 HIS PRECIOUS BLOOD

"But with the precious blood of Christ, as of a lamb without blemish and without spot" (1 Peter 1:19)

Jesus shed his blood on the cross for our sake that we may have everlasting life provided we believe in him. His blood shed was precious, without blemish and without any spot. As was the blood of Jesus precious so was He Himself to the Father and to those who believe in him. Jesus was the living stone, who was rejected by men, but chosen of God.

Speaking at the Lord's Supper Jesus Christ says about remembering his death. Lord Jesus says that unless we eat the emblems that represent his flesh and drink from the cup that represents his blood we have no life. We were once far off but are brought near to his presence by the blood of Christ. We are able to enter in his most holy place by the blood of Christ.

Lord Jesus Christ is the mediator of the new covenant and to the blood of sprinkling that speaks of better things than that of Abel. Our fellowship with one another is sustained when we walk in the light just as he was in the light. The blood of Jesus Christ cleanses us from all our sins. He washed us from our sins in his own blood. (Ref. John 6:53, Ephesians 2:13, Hebrews 10:19, Hebrews 12:24, Hebrews 13:20, 1 John 1:7, Revelation 1:5)

"To whom coming, as unto a living stone, disallowed indeed of men, but chosen of God, and precious" (1 Peter

2:4 – (Cf. Ps 118:22; Isaiah 28:16; 53:5))

Peter wrote "Wherefore also it is contained in the scripture, Behold, I lay in Sion a chief corner stone, elect, precious: and he that believeth on him shall not be confounded" (1 Peter 2:6).

For those who reject Lord Jesus Christ as savior he is a stone of stumbling, a rock of offence, and they will get hurt, but we are redeemed with precious blood of Lord Jesus Christ and not by corruptible things such as silver and gold and, therefore, we are as lively stones are built up spiritual house, an holy priesthood to offer spiritual sacrifices, acceptable to God by Jesus Christ.

"And a stone of stumbling, and a rock of offence, even to them which stumble at the word, being disobedient: whereunto also they were appointed" (1 Peter 2:8).

DAY 17 THE LAMB THAT WAS SLAIN

"For when we were yet without strength, in due time Christ died for the ungodly" (Romans 5:6)

Jesus had embarrassing situations earlier when Jews tried to harm Him, but no one could do any harm to him, because the due time for Him to die on behalf of us had not yet come (Ref. John 7:30). Until the determined hour was come no one could do any harm to Jesus, and when the appointed hour was come, He was taken into custody by the chief priests and elders who took counsel against Him to put Him to death.

"And Jesus answered them, saying, The hour is come, that the Son of man should be glorified" (John 12:23)

The events on the day of trial, as before the trial, and after the trial of Jesus, and the plan of man's redemption were determined by the eternal counsel of the Almighty God.

"And all that dwell upon the earth shall worship him, whose names are not written in the book of life of the Lamb slain from the foundation of the world" (Revelation 13:8)

All the disciples of Jesus scattered away, from the scene when Jesus was arrested, and left Him all alone in fulfillment of the prophecy by the prophet Zechariah. (Ref. Zechariah 13:7). Peter denied Jesus three times in fulfillment of the prophecy from Jesus. Judas Iscariot betrayed Jesus in fulfillment of the prophecy by the prophet Zechariah (Ref. Zechariah 11:12-13)

"Awake, O sword, against my shepherd, and against the man that is my fellow, saith the LORD of hosts: smite the shepherd, and the sheep shall be scattered: and I will turn mine hand upon the little ones" (Zechariah 13:7)

While Peter repented and chose to serve the Lord, Judas Iscariot betrayed Jesus and committed suicide.

DAY 18 JUDAS ISCARIOT BETRAYS

Jesus chose twelve disciples for Him but one of them turned out to be betrayer. After Jesus ended His prayer in Gethsemane, Judas Iscariot, one of the twelve, came along with a great multitude of people, who were sent by chief priests and elders, with swords and staves. Judas Iscariot gave sign to the accompanying multitude that whosoever he kisses was Jesus, and that they could hold him fast.

The prophecy of the betrayal of Jesus, mentioned in the Old Testament, was fulfilled when Judas Iscariot betrayed Him (Ref. Matthew 27:9).

"And I said unto them, If ye think good, give me my price; and if not, forbear. So they weighed for my price thirty pieces of silver. And the LORD said unto me, Cast it unto the potter: a goodly price that I was prised at of them. And I took the thirty pieces of silver, and cast them to the potter in the house of the LORD" (Zechariah 11:12-13)

Lord Jesus came into this world in the form of servant and in the likeness of man to redeem mankind from sin, but His price was determined as thirty pieces of silver. When Judas Iscariot received thirty pieces of silver the prophecy in the Old Testament was fulfilled.

Exodus Chapter 21:28-32 contain instructions as to how payment of compensation was to be made if an ox hurts man or woman. If by such hurting a man or woman dies, the ox was to be surely be killed by stoning; and its flesh shall not be eaten. By doing so, the owner of the ox is set free. However, if the ox pushed a man or woman with its horn, and if the person died, not immediately, but subsequently, the ox was to be stoned to death, and in addition the owner of the ox also was to be put to death. If a manservant or maidservant was pushed by the ox, the owner of the ox was to give the master of the manservant or maidservant thirty shekels of silver, and the ox was to be stoned.

Thus the value of the manservant or maidservant was determined to be thirty pieces of silver. This is how the price of betraying Jesus by Judas Iscariot was determined.

"Who, being in the form of God, thought it not robbery to be equal with God: But made himself of no reputation, and took upon him the form of a servant, and was made in the likeness of men" (Philippians 2:6-7)

God in His providence determined that the thirty pieces of silver used for betrayal of Jesus Christ, by Judas Iscariot, to be used for salvation of Gentiles, when that amount was used for purchase of a land, where dead bodies of Gentiles were buried. (Ref. Matt. 27:3-10)

John in his vision saw such provision for Gentiles...

"But the court which is without the temple leave out, and measure it not; for it is given unto the Gentiles: and the holy city shall they tread under foot forty and two months" (Revelation 11:2)

Jews held Gentiles in contempt and allotted the "Potter's field", which was also called "Aceldama", and considered it as the fittest place for burying strangers who came to Jerusalem and died.

"And it was known unto all the dwellers at Jerusalem; insomuch as that field is called in their proper tongue, Aceldama, that is to say, The field of blood" (Acts 1:19)

Judas Iscariot committed suicide as recorded in Acts Chapter 1:15-20 where Peter, the Apostle, declared that the prophecy was fulfilled. Judas Iscariot fell headlong and his bowels gushed out when he burst asunder. Peter's assertion was also based on Psalm 69:26 and Psalm 109:8

DAY 19 THE TRIAL OF JESUS

The chief priests and the elders of the people delivered Jesus in the morning to the governor, Pontius Pilate, for executing Jesus to death. If only they said Jesus violated their religious laws, Pilate would have let Jesus go even before the trial began, because Roman Government had no authority to deal with cases related to religious laws. Knowing this well, the Jews leveled false charges against Jesus; and the charges were related to treason, insurrection against Government.

It was only few years ago before the crucifixion of Jesus that Roman Government stripped Jews from their power to inflict Capital punishment on those who broke their religious laws. It was because they did not have any powers over Him, neither did Roman Government, unless they were given from heaven above, no one by his power could execute Jesus.

Ultimately, after the trial of Jesus was over, He was found innocent. There was nothing, He did in His lifetime, which made Him worthy of death penalty. Even secular law provides chance for the accused to be acquitted of unproved charges, but in the case of Jesus, Pontius Pilate, who boasted that he had the power to execute or release Jesus, delivered innocent Jesus to be crucified.

Because it was the purpose of Jesus to die for men in their stead, He did not plead for his innocence or acquittal.

All that Jesus did was good for mankind; such as healing the sick, casting away the devils from those who were afflicted by them. He taught repentance and the way to receive everlasting life.

The chief priests, the Jews and the elders of people feared that Jesus would become prominent among them, and would replace them in power. Therefore, they leveled false charges against Him and were determined to see that He was put to death. They even cried that the blood of Jesus to be upon them and their children. Pilate found no fault in Jesus.

Pilate's wife was troubled in a dream about the illegal trial of Jesus and cautioned him; yet he delivered Jesus into their hands to do what they desired to do.

The last attempt Pilate made was to release either a criminal, named Barabbas or Jesus according to their choice, and they preferred Barabbas to be released instead of Jesus.

What a choice they made! They preferred to kill Jesus, who was good to them all His life, and to be robbed by Barabbas, the criminal. They made a choice that the blood of Jesus to be on them, and their children, at the cost of some secular benefits. They preferred lies instead of truth saying Jesus resorted to insurrection.

"The Son of man" would have gone as it was written about Him, but the tragedy was that they invited troubles for them, and preferred to receive punishment from God.

It is not that we loved God first but He loved us first, and that is the reason why He sent His one and only begotten Son into this world to die in our stead. He died for our sake and was buried. His body did not see corruption and He rose on the third day and after forty days He ascended into heaven.

"And being found in fashion as a man, he humbled himself, and became obedient unto death, even the death of the cross". (Philippians 2:8)

DAY 20 ROLE OF SATAN AT THE CROSS

At the time of Jesus' crucifixion, Satan knew of the curse that God pronounced on him for deceiving Eve and Adam in the Garden of Eden (Genesis 3:14-15). The Legion in the man affected with evil spirits acknowledged that Jesus was the Son God (Mark 5:7-9).

Satan knew that the Son of God, Jesus, the seed of the woman, will crush his head while he attempts to bruise his heel. The victory belonged to Jesus and as it was evident Lord Jesus Christ defeated Satan at the cross, and thus paid price for our sin, in order that whosoever confesses his/her sin to Him, shall not perish, but have everlasting life. However, Satan was ignorant of the fact that the death, burial and resurrection of Jesus would bring Salvation to man.

Satan's main aim was to get Jesus out of his way. He tried to kill Jesus by Herod the great, who desired to have information about Jesus from Magi when they were going to worship Jesus.

Satan was not successful there because Joseph and Mary departed with child Jesus to Egypt at the behest of the angel of the Lord. Satan tried to defeat Jesus by tempting Him but he failed in his attempts. He tried to harm Jesus through scribes and Pharisees, but none of them could do any harm to Him until the hour for Jesus to lay down His life by His choice at the will of the Father came by.

"Then Herod, when he saw that he was mocked of the wise men, was exceeding wroth, and sent forth, and slew all the children that were in Bethlehem, and in all the coasts thereof, from two years old and under, according to the time which he had diligently enquired of the wise men" Matthew 2:16

Satan's endeavors were always evil and towards destroying man. If only he knew that the death, burial and resurrection would have brought salvation to mankind, he would never have played a role in Jesus reaching the cross and dying on it for the redemption of mankind.

In all the attempts made by Satan, he was unsuccessful to achieve his purposes because God has the ultimate control. Satan was powerless to hold back Jesus achieving His purposes. Scribes and Pharisees desired to see a sign from Jesus but He said to them.

"For as Jonas was three days and three nights in the whale's belly; so shall the Son of man be three days and three nights in the heart of the earth". Matthew 12:40

None of them understood that Jesus was referring to His death, burial and resurrection. Likewise, when Jesus said, "...Destroy this temple, and in three days I will raise it up" (John 2:19), neither Jews who sold merchandize at the temple, nor His disciples understood what Jesus said. Jews were wondering how Jesus could build the temple in three days, when in fact, it took forty six years to build it.

Nevertheless, Jesus spoke of the temple of His body. In fact, those who crucified Jesus mocked at Him saying:

"...Thou that destroyest the temple, and buildest [it] in three days, save thyself. If thou be the Son of God, come down from the cross" Matthew 27:40

The disciples, who heard Jesus, say that He would raise the temple up in three days, did not understand Jesus when He said those words, but they remembered after resurrection of Jesus (Ref. John 2:22).

DAY 21 PURPOSES OF GOD PREVAIL

Satan is given freedom to be the ruler of this world until his time ends; however, all the events in the world are controlled by God and nothing that happens in the world happens without His knowledge. Satan cannot overstep God achieving His purposes.

Considering the fact that Satan was not permitted to touch the life of Job, it can be inferred that Satan has no power over the life of man. Satan keeps looking for opportunity to strike man and he plays havoc in the life of man, when he finds that man is left all alone by himself without the help of God. How that man is left by himself without the help of God?

It is as simple as man choosing to leave God and rejecting His help continuously. God allows man to choose his way to salvation, but his choice, again was in the knowledge of God. However, when man continuously chooses to rebel against God's ways, It is then that God hands him over to his choice (Cf. Romans 1:26-32)

The wicked wife of Ahab introduced Baal worship in the Northern Province of Israel. Ahab desired Naboth's vineyard, and Jezebel devised cunning plan, and grabbed the vineyard. Prophet Elijah the Tishbite prophesied their ruin and eventually their blood was licked by dogs.

Ahab, the king of Israel, made a league with Jehoshaphat,

King of Judah, and ventured to capture Ramothgilead, which was a strong city east of Jordan in Gad's territory. However, Jehoshaphat desired that Ahab consult prophets. Ahab consulted his own prophets who gave a pleasing reply that he can go and capture Ramothgilead.

Again, Jehoshaphat asked Ahab to consult a prophet of the LORD, if there is one, nearby. Ahab knew of one Micaiah, a prophet of God, who always gave bad report to him. Ahab was forced into sending word for him to come and prophesy. In the meanwhile Zedekiah, a prophet, came with iron horns on his head and said: "Thus saith the LORD, With these shalt thou push the Syrians, until thou have consumed them" (1 Kings 22:11b).

Ahab desired to hear good prophesy from Miciah but the latter said: "… As the LORD liveth, what the LORD saith unto me, that will I speak. (1 Kings 22:14b). Miciah sarcastically said to Ahab to go and capture Ramothgilead, but when Ahab insisted on him to speak the truth, Miciah said he saw all Israel scattered upon the hills as if the sheep had no shepherd and, therefore, everyone in Israel should return to their home in peace, which is to say Ahab would be defeated in the battle.

Ahab said in contempt to Jehoshaphat that he anticipated bad prophecy from Miciah.

"And the king of Israel said unto Jehoshaphat, Did I not tell thee that he would prophesy no good concerning me, but evil? (1 Kings 22:18)

Then, Miciah explains how he saw the LORD sitting on His throne and all the host of heaven stood by Him on His right hand and on His left hand.

The prophet saw the LORD asking his host of heaven, as to who will persuade Ahab that he may go and fight against Ramothgilead, and the angels gave one opinion after another. In the meanwhile, a spirit came and stood before the LORD and said "I will go forth, and I will be a lying spirit in the mouth of all his prophets" and the LORD said "Thou shalt persuade him, and prevail also: go forth, and do so" (Cf. 1 Kings 22:21-22)

Ahab was very angry with Miciah because he did not prophecy according to his desire, and imprisoned Miciah and afflicted him. However, Ahab eventually got killed in the battle, thus fulfilling God's purposes.

DAY 22 BLIND FROM BIRTH HEALED

"Wherefore, as by one man sin entered into the world, and death by sin; and so death passed upon all men, for that all have sinned" (Romans 5:12)

While Jews thought of doing harm to Jesus after a fierce argument over His authority to forgive sins and heal the sick, He left the Temple unharmed, which proves that He was not only human in all respects but He was divine, as well. After leaving the temple He saw a man born blind, and took compassion on him even before he asked for favor. It seems there was a belief during the days of Jesus that spirits waited for body, and they that were born with deformities in their bodies were those who sinned when they were in spirit form. Those beliefs are heresies.

If spirits committed sin and took the form of body, every spirit, having committed sin would take similar deformity in his body-form. A child in the mother's womb cannot commit sin and take a deformity in its body at birth; but everyone is sinner by virtue of being the offspring of Adam.

It is within the knowledge of God as to the purpose and the kind of deformity a child is born with. Man is not supposed to make guess-work. God has revealed to man what is necessary for him to live a life of peace in Him, and He kept other things secret for Himself.

"The secret things belong unto the LORD our God: but those things which are revealed belong unto us and to our children for ever, that we may do all the words of this law" (Deuteronomy 29:29)

The belief that spirits wait for bodies and occupy bodies is heresy, and it contradicts what the Bible says. God created man out of dust and sin entered into the world as a consequence of Eve and Adam transgressing the commandment of God. That sin from Adam was passed onto all mankind.

It is not because the spirits committed sin that they had the deformities in their bodies, but it is because the sin was passed on from Adam to everyone in the world that everyone has to be redeemed of one's sin.

Thus by "one man sin entered into the world, and death by sin; and death passed upon all men". Every individual, therefore, needs to be reconciled unto God.

"For as by one man's disobedience many were made sinners, so by the obedience of one shall many be made righteous" (Romans 5:19)

There is no one who is righteous and all have sinned and come short of the glory of God. Everyone needs savior and without one's sins are forgiven one will have his eternity in the 'lake of fire', but the gift of God is salvation and whosoever believes in Jesus shall have everlasting life.

"For all have sinned, and come short of the glory of God"

(Romans 3:23)

"All we like sheep have gone astray; we have turned every one to his own way; and the LORD hath laid on him the iniquity of us all" (Isaiah 53:6)

The disciples questioned Jesus as to who sinned in the case of the man who was born blind; was it his parents, or he himself? Jesus answered and said neither his parents sinned nor he sinned, but that the works of the Father should be manifest in him. However, we are not supposed to make suppositions that every man born with deformity is made to be born in order to bring glory to the Father.

Then, Jesus went on to say that He has to do the works of the Father, and after having said thus he healed the man born blind from his birth.

"If we say that we have no sin, we deceive ourselves, and the truth is not in us. If we confess our sins, he is faithful and just to forgive us our sins, and to cleanse us from all unrighteousness. If we say that we have not sinned, we make him a liar, and his word is not in us" (1 John 1:8-10)

DAY 23 TESTIMONY OF THE BLIND MAN

"I must work the works of him that sent me, while it is day: the night cometh, when no man can work. As long as I am in the world, I am the light of the world" (John 9:4-5)

Jesus answered the question, from His disciples as to whether it was because of the blind man's sin from birth or the sin of his parents that he was born blind, saying that the man was blind not because of his sin or of his parents but that the works of the Father may be glorified in him. He said, it was apt that He should heal him, because the dark days are ahead soon. He affirmed that as long as He was in this world, He was the light of the world.

While the Pharisees watched if Jesus healed him on the Sabbath day, He not only healed the blind man but he made clay on the ground from His spit. He, then, applied the clay to the eyes of the blind man, and then said to him to go and wash his eyes in the pool of Siloam. Jesus was clearly showing that if the work involved on Sabbath day is for doing good for somebody it is not a violation of Sabbath command.

The man's neighbors wondered and watched with surprise that he, who was blind from his birth, was able to see with his eyes. Some of them accepted the fact that he was the same blind man, while some others did not believe that he was the same man; but the blind man boldly acknowledged that it was he who was blind.

On inquiry the blind man gave a testimony that a man named Jesus made clay on the ground with his spit, and applied it to his eyes, and then said to him to go and wash in the pool of Siloam. He continued saying that he obeyed the command from Jesus, and went washed his eyes in the pool of Siloam, and thereby he was healed. On further inquiry as to where Jesus was; he said he did not know where He was.

The blind man, who was healed, was brought before the Pharisees because Jesus healed him on the Sabbath day. They were curious to know who healed him. They never saw anyone born blind receive sight, and, therefore, argued within themselves and some said Jesus was from God, and some said He was not from God because He did not keep the Sabbath Command.

This difference of opinion brought division among them and they questioned the man as to what he thought about Jesus. The man said He was a prophet. His thinking was apt because until then Prophets came and spoke the word of God. Jesus was not only Prophet, Priest, King but He was the Son of God. Many prophets came until then, of whom John the Baptist was the last one, and Jesus was the Son of God, the very God Himself.

"God, who at sundry times and in divers manners spake in time past unto the fathers by the prophets, Hath in these last days spoken unto us by his Son, whom he hath appointed heir of all things, by whom also he made the worlds; Who being the brightness of his glory, and the express image of his person, and upholding all things by the word of his power, when he had by himself purged our sins, sat down on the right hand of the Majesty on high" (Hebrews 1:1-3)

Lord Jesus Christ was the only begotten of the Father and was sent into this world to save sinners. He had the power to forgive sins. He forgave the man with Palsy at the Bethesda pool, and he forgave the prostitute woman, who was caught red-handed when she was sinning. Jews did not understand that He was the Messiah. Pharisees, Sadducees and Scribes were always after Him to find fault with Him and to harm Him.

The man answered Jews and explained to them with much patience as to how Jesus healed him, yet they did not believe in his assertion. How much God loved the children of Israel, and yet they rejected Jesus as their Messiah.

"O Jerusalem, Jerusalem, thou that killest the prophets, and stonest them which are sent unto thee, how often would I have gathered thy children together, even as a hen gathereth her chickens under her wings, and ye would not!" (Matthew 23:37)

DAY 24 THE FATHER AND THE SON

"His parents answered them and said, We know that this is our son, and that he was born blind" John 9:20

The blind man, who was healed, answered Pharisees, according to his knowledge that the man, who healed him, was a prophet. However, Jews did not believe concerning the man that was healed, and they called his parents to identify their son, if he was truly theirs. Answering the question from the Jews, the parents of the man not only identified the man as their son, but also testified that he was born blind.

Pharisees were a powerful lobby among the Jews and they could cast out anyone from the synagogues, if one violated their instructions, or spoke against God, or acknowledged that Jesus was the Christ. Therefore, the parents of the man said to the Jews that they may direct their questions to the man himself, because he was grown up and is of age. They said they did not know by what miracle their son received vision.

Pharisees called the man once again and admonished him to praise God and accused that Jesus was sinner. They believed the words of Moses written in Pentateuch, (the first five books of Jewish and Christian Scriptures in the Old Testament), that the LORD God is one LORD and, therefore, rejected Jesus as their Messiah.

"Hear, O Israel: The LORD our God [is] one LORD" Deuteronomy 6:4

Indeed, the LORD our God is one LORD, but they did not understand the fact that Jesus was incarnate God and the LORD Himself, in the form of servant, and in the likeness of man. How sad it is that Jews understood Jesus as sinner, in spite of seeing miracles, signs and wonders from Him. They already had intense argument over this point earlier, as we read in John Chapter 5:20-30, where Jesus identified Himself with the Father.

Jesus said Father loves the Son, and as the Father resurrects the dead, the Son will quicken those whom he wishes to. The Father does not judge anyone but entire power is given to the Son, and it is the Son, who judges. When Jesus later, as we read in John 10:30, said that He and the Father are one, none understood him clearly. The Jews took up stones to kill Him.

It is hard, indeed, for those who are not deep in their understanding to be convinced of the fact that Jesus was the savior of the world; not merely a Prophet, but He was Prophet, Priest, King of kings, born of the Virgin Mary, the Son of God, and the very God Himself incarnate in the likeness of man. He dwelt among men, died on the cross, bearing our sin, our shame in order that we may believe and receive everlasting life.

More than seven hundred years before Jesus was born Isaiah, the prophet, prophesied about Jesus as follows:

"For unto us a child is born, unto us a son is given: and the government shall be upon his shoulder: and his name shall be called Wonderful, Counsellor, The mighty God, The everlasting Father, The Prince of Peace". (Isaiah 9:6)

Apostle Paul wrote:

"But made himself of no reputation, and took upon him the form of a servant, and was made in the likeness of men: And being found in fashion as a man, he humbled himself, and became obedient unto death, even the death of the cross. Wherefore God also hath highly exalted him, and given him a name which is above every name: That at the name of Jesus every knee should bow, of [things] in heaven, and [things] in earth, and [things] under the earth; And [that] every tongue should confess that Jesus Christ [is] Lord, to the glory of God the Father". Philippians 2:7-11

Lord Jesus Christ said:

"Verily, verily, I say unto you, He that heareth my word, and believeth on him that sent me, hath everlasting life, and shall not come into condemnation; but is passed from death unto life" John 5:24.

DAY 25 GLIMSPE OF RESURRECTION

"So when this corruptible shall have put on incorruption, and this mortal shall have put on immortality, then shall be brought to pass the saying that is written, Death is swallowed up in victory. O death, where is thy sting? O grave, where is thy victory?" (1 Corinthians 15:54-55)

There was a woman, named Mary, who came to Jesus, when he sat for a meal in the house of Simon the leper, at Bethany. She opened an alabaster box of ointment of spikenard; broke open the box and poured on His head, the precious ointment, which was very expensive.

Some among those who saw the woman pouring the precious ointment on Jesus' head spoke in indignation, saying she wasted the ointment, which was worth more than three hundred pence (roughly about $41.40). They murmured that the money could have been given to poor. Jesus perceived their thoughts and said poor are always with them, but He was not going to be with them physically always. Commending her action that it signified His death and burial, He said she will be remembered wherever the gospel was preached. (Ref. Mark 14:4-9, John 11:2)

Mary had a sister named Martha and a brother named Lazarus. Once when Lazarus was sick Mary and Martha sent word to Jesus seeking His help. When Jesus heard about the sickness of Lazarus He said that the sickness in

Lazarus was not unto death but it was for the glory of God, and that the Son of God might be glorified thereby. Sickness could be the result of sin in a man, or for the glory of God.

After Jesus healing the man at the pool at Bethesda He saw the man in the temple and warned Him that he should not sin anymore; otherwise worse could happen to him. This shows that the sickness in that man was because of his sin, but in the case of Lazarus, and in another case, where a blind man restored, Jesus said that the sickness in them was for the glory of God, that the Son of God might be glorified thereby.

Even after hearing that Lazarus was sick Jesus stayed where he was and then left for Bethany after two days via Judea. When he was in Bethany it was already four days past since Lazarus was dead and was buried. Martha believed that Lazarus would rise in resurrection at the last day, but Jesus said to her that He was the resurrection, and the life, and whoever believed in Him, shall live.

"Jesus said unto her, I am the resurrection, and the life: he that believeth in me, though he were dead, yet shall he live" (John 11:25)

The departure of Lazarus from this earth was painful to Mary and Martha; however they were comforted greatly by Jesus who shared their grief, by weeping along with them, before showing the miracle.

"Jesus wept". (John 11:35)

John 11:35 is the shortest verse in the Bible. However, it brings out great truth about the humanity of Jesus. He wept and shared their grief. Jesus was fully divine and fully human when He was on this earth.

Jesus raised Lazarus from his death. Some people left the scene in unbelief, while many Jews believed in Jesus. It is evident that Lazarus was raised in his body only to die again, but when God the Father raised Jesus from the dead, His body did not see corruption, and He had the body which could pass closed doors, and appear and disappear at His will, at any place He desired to be instantaneously.

Apostle Paul by the revelation of Jesus Christ writes, in 1 Corinthians Chapter 15, about the death of believers and their resurrection. He writes that the bodies of dead in Christ shall be changed, in a moment in the twinkling of an eye, into incorruptible immortal bodies, when the "...Lord himself shall descend from heaven with a shout, with the voice of the archangel, and with the trump of God: and the dead in Christ shall rise first: Then we which are alive and remain shall be caught up together with them in the clouds, to meet the Lord in the air: and so shall we ever be with the Lord". (1 Thessalonians 4:16-17)

When the dead in Christ rise from the dead they sing..." O grave, where is thy victory?" and those who are caught up be meet the Lord in the air, will sing..." O death, where is thy sting?"

DAY 26 DISPUTE WITH PHARISEES

"Then again called they the man that was blind, and said unto him, Give God the praise: we know that this man is a sinner" (John 9:24)

Pharisees called Jesus a sinner on the pretext that He healed on the Sabbath day, a man, who was born blind. The man answered Pharisees and said he did not know whether or not Jesus was sinner; but one thing he knew was that he was blind before and now he has vision to see.

The Pharisees were curious to know the details again. The man already explained to them very clearly that Jesus spat on the ground, made clay and applied it to his eyes, and because he obeyed the command from Jesus, and went and washed his eyes in the pool of Siloam, he was healed. Now, when the Jews asked him second time, he got annoyed at them and said "I have told you already, and ye did not hear".

How often we listen to someone and yet, we desire the same to be reiterated, because of either unbelief or hesitate to accept the truth. The Pharisees resorted to similar attitude when they asked the man second time as to how he was healed. The man wondered and asked them if it was because they want to become the disciples of Jesus that they want to hear about the miraculous healing again.

When they heard the man speak in contempt they reviled at him saying he was the disciple of Jesus, and they were of Moses. They ridiculed saying God spoke to them through Moses but as for Jesus, they did not know who He was, and where He came from. The man had a dig at them saying even though they did not know where Jesus came from, and who He was, yet they marveled at His works. The man, who was born blind, was healed by the Lord, and he spoke words of wisdom than do Pharisees, who were considered to be the wise men of the day.

The man said since the world began not one incident was heard by anyone of the kind of healing that Jesus did in him. He boldly testified that if Jesus were not of God, He could have not have done anything.

Pharisees were raged in anger and cast him out of their fellowship accusing him that he was born in sins and asked him how is that he ventured to teach them. They, who were in sins, judged the man that he was born in sins.

"And why beholdest thou the mote that is in thy brother's eye, but considerest not the beam that is in thine own eye?" (Matthew 7:3)

Jesus finding the man asked him if he believed on the Son of God, and the man wondered who the Son of God was. Then Jesus said to him that the man has seen Him, and He, who was talking to him, was the Son of God. The man called Jesus as "Lord", which is to say "Master", and said that he believed that Jesus was the Son of God, and worshipped Him.

DAY 27 BLIND SEE

"Jesus said unto them, If ye were blind, ye should have no sin: but now ye say, We see; therefore your sin remaineth" (John 9:41)

Jesus said to the man, who was healed of his blindness that blind see and perceive who He was, but those who have sight will be like blind. He judges in order to see that those, who have eyes, may not see, and those, who are blind, may see the truth.

Some of the Pharisees heard the fierce words spoken by Jesus concerning them, and they countered Him, and asked Him if they were blind. Then, Jesus replied saying, it would have been better if they were blind and not see rather than have eyes and not see the truth. If they said that they were blind their sins would have been forgiven, but because they were boasting that they have eyes their sin remains in them.

Apostle Paul writes about Mosaic Law, which the Pharisees were very conversant, and attempted to keep in vain. The Law pointed to the guilt of a person, but it never provided salvation; and surprisingly, Jews, and likewise some in the present generation, try to keep the Law in vain, instead of depending on the grace of our Lord Jesus Christ, and fail miserably in both the cases.

Neither they are able to fulfill the conditions of Mosaic Law, nor do they make attempts to come under the grace of our Lord Jesus Christ. They try to be blind to the truth, and lose sight of the light, and the glorious things that are visible in the light.

"Now we know that what things soever the law saith, it saith to them who are under the law: that every mouth may be stopped, and all the world may become guilty before God. Therefore by the deeds of the law there shall no flesh be justified in his sight: for by the law is the knowledge of sin" (Romans 3:19-20)

The creator is greater than creation. Worship the creator than the creation. Moses was creation of God and he was a servant of God. Jesus was greater than Moses. Therefore, let us boast in the cleansing power of the blood of Lord Jesus Christ, rather than boasting in Moses.

The LORD gave the Law to the children of Israel though Moses, his servant, and because they failed to keep the Law, Jesus came into the world to die for all sinners that by His grace everyone, who confesses Him as the Lord, and believes in heart that God raised Him from the dead, may become righteous. Salvation belongs to Lord Jesus Christ and it is by Him alone that one receives everlasting life.

"For this man was counted worthy of more glory than Moses, inasmuch as he who hath builded the house hath more honour than the house. For every house is builded by some man; but he that built all things is God. And Moses verily was faithful in all his house, as a servant, for a testimony of those things which were to be spoken after; But Christ as a son over his own house; whose house are we, if we hold fast the confidence and the rejoicing of the hope firm unto the end" (Hebrews 3:3-6)

DAY 28 DEATH OR SLEEP

"When Jesus heard that, he said, This sickness is not unto death, but for the glory of God, that the Son of God might be glorified thereby" (John 11:4)

Lord Jesus made a stunning statement before His disciples that He would go to Bethany and wake up Lazarus out of sleep. Mary, Martha and Lazarus were friends of Jesus. At the first report He received from Mary and Martha that their brother Lazarus was sick, Jesus said that the sickness in Lazarus was not unto his death, but for the glory of God. He tarried for two more days at the place where He was, and then said to His disciples that He would to go Judea.

When Jesus heard that Lazarus was sick, He said that the sickness in Lazarus was not unto death, but the latter suffered it, in order that the glory of the Son of God may be manifest to all. Jesus loved Lazarus, and his sisters Mary and Martha.

Jesus was sure of His work on the earth and that He had to fulfill the will of the Father. He refused to answer quickly on three occasions.

Once when, Mary, the earthly mother of Jesus, requested Him to help the host of the marriage at Cana. Second time, when the mother of Zebedee's children came to Him with her sons, and prayed that her two sons may be granted the privilege to sit, one on His right hand, and other on the left, in His kingdom. Third time, it was when Mary and Martha, sisters of Lazarus requested help from Jesus when their brother was sick. However, He answered the first request and the third request according to the timing of Father and His time. The second request was in the power of the Father to grant and not in His power, and, therefore, He said:

"...to sit on my right hand, and on my left, is not mine to give, but it shall be given to them for whom it is prepared of my Father" (Matthew 20:23b)

In spite of the disciples of Jesus pointing to Him about the impending danger, He chose to go to Judea, where Jews waited to kill Him. Jesus questioned them if there were no twelve hours in a day! Jesus was, obviously pointing to them about the availability of limited time at his disposal to fulfill the will of the Father, even if it involved danger to His life. He also knew that no one can do any harm to Him before His hour came.

Jesus explained to them that a man, who walks in the day, does not stumble because he sees the light of the world. On the contrary, he, who walks in the night, stumbles because of absence of light in him.

Jesus, having replied His disciples their question, in a way perhaps not clearly understood by them, surprised them with another statement that Lazarus, their friend, was sleeping, and He would go and awake him out of sleep. The disciples of Jesus, who were surprised to hear from Him that Lazarus was sleeping, thought, indeed the latter was sleeping, and was in good health; but Jesus spoke of the death of Lazarus.

The truth was that in the sight of Lord Jesus Christ, the Son of God, Lazarus was sleeping, but in the sight of men, he was dead.

God knows all things and He does everything according to His will and His purpose. Lazarus was raised and the Father's name was glorified through Jesus, the Son of God.

"And we know that all things work together for good to them that love God, to them who are the called according to his purpose" (Romans 8:28)

DAY 29 MARTHA BELIEVED

Jesus and His disciples decided to go to Bethany, where Mary and Martha waited for Him, seeking His intervention, when their brother Lazarus was sick. Jesus knew that Lazarus was dead even before he left for Judea from the place where He was.

Just before Jesus left for Bethany from Judea, He said to His disciples, that He was glad that He was not at Bethany. He delayed in order that He may bring glory to the Father, and thereby those who watched may believe in Him. He was sure of bringing back Lazarus to life. When Jesus came into Bethany along with His disciples, it was already four days since the dead body of Lazarus was in the grave.

Bethany was fifteen furlongs away from Jerusalem, and many Jews came to Martha and Mary to comfort them, after the death of Lazarus. Obviously, this shows that Mary, Martha and Lazarus were very popular in Bethany, and they had very good friends, who had close fellowship with them.

When Martha heard that Jesus was coming to their home, she went out, and met Him where He was. Mary, who perhaps was disappointed at the death of her brother, sat still at home. Martha was enthusiastic, and had zeal for the Lord. Her brother's death did not prevent her from meeting Jesus. She said to Jesus that if He were present at their home, when Lazarus was sick, the latter would not have died. Her faith was great that, even in those trying circumstances, Jesus would be able to bring some good for them, by praying to God, who, as she believed, will surely answer His prayers.

"Then said Martha unto Jesus, Lord, if thou hadst been here, my brother had not died" (John 11:21)

Jesus assured Martha that her brother, Lazarus would rise again. However, she thought in a different way that Lazarus would arise from the death at the last day. Then, Jesus said...

"...I am the resurrection, and the life: he that believeth in me, though he were dead, yet shall he live" John 11:25

We were all dead in trespasses but He has quickened us and promised us everlasting life. Even though we walked according to the course of this world, obeying the prince of the power of the air, "fulfilling the desires of the flesh and of the mind", God in His mercy loved us, and gave salvation to us, in response to our yielding to the pleasures of our Lord Jesus Christ, and accepting Him as our Savior. (Ref. Ephesians 2:1-6)

Martha said she believed that Jesus was the Christ, the Son of God, who was to come into the world as prophesied in the Old Testament Scriptures.

It is time for those, who have not believed in Jesus, to take time to repent, and turn to Lord Jesus Christ. Believe Jesus is the Lord, and that He was raised from the dead. Death has no victory over a believer in Christ.

DAY 30 THE FELLOWSHIP

"Jesus wept" (John 11:35)

After Martha acknowledged that Jesus was the resurrection, and the life, and that He was the Christ, the Son of God, who was to come according to prophecies in the Old Testament, she was comforted within herself, and, thereafter, not sitting quite to watch as to what Jesus was about to do, she ran to her home and whispered in the ears of her sister, Mary, that Jesus was coming to the town.

Martha's belief and assertion were extremely commendable, for she not only gave testimony about Jesus, but she ran to tell her sister about the Lord. Her Lord was the Christ, the Son of God, who came into the world according to the prophecies. Her Lord comforted that her brother, who was dead for four days then, would rise again.

Now, when Mary heard from her sister that their friend Jesus was coming to the town, she ran to Him, not taking cognizance of the Jews, who were in the home, comforting her after the death of Lazarus. It was a solemn occasion, when friends of Mary, Martha and Lazarus, were in their home, sharing their grief, and yet, the arrival of their Lord, was greater to her than any occasion. Mary left home, immediately she came to know about the Lord, and met Him where He was.

The Jews, who were in their home, comforting them, thought Mary ran to the tomb, to weep over his brother, Lazarus. The Jews, who comforted her at home, also went to the place where Mary went and continued comforting her. Obviously, the fellowship Mary, Martha and Lazarus, had with the Jews at Bethany was great. They not only comforted Martha and Mary at their home, but also followed Mary, when she ran to see Jesus.

On seeing the Lord, Mary's immediate complaint was similar to that of her sister, Martha, who said earlier that if Jesus were present at their home, when Lazarus was sick, their brother would not have died.

"Then when Mary was come where Jesus was, and saw him, she fell down at his feet, saying unto him, Lord, if thou hadst been here, my brother had not died" (John 11:32)

The Lord saw Mary and also the Jews, who were with her, weeping. Filled with humanity, Jesus groaned in spirit and was troubled within Him, depicting His great love towards the needy and sorrowful. Jesus shared their grief at the grave of Lazarus and He wept. The Jews marveled at the love Jesus had towards the family. The Lord loved the family, who loved their Master.

The family of Lazarus had very close fellowship with one another, and yet Jesus came to the tomb of Lazarus after four days of his death, because His priority was to bring glory the Father in heaven, and also to see that His disciples and others have greater increase in faith when He does an exceptional miracle.

His priority was to speak about the kingdom of heaven at Judea on His way to Bethany. He knew that He would surely raise Lazarus, but before that He had some obligations to fulfill. That is the reason why He questioned His disciples as to whether there were no twelve hours in the day. The Jews knew the importance of accomplishing their tasks within twelve hours of the day, and Jesus was on this earth with a definite task from the Father, to fulfill within the limited time that He had at His disposal.

It is very important that we have fellowship and comfort in the Lord, one another in sorrows and painful situations.

Wishing Grace in the name of Jesus Christ, Apostle Paul writes to the Church of God at Corinth that God will confirm them unto the end that they may be blameless, and then asserts that "God is faithful, by whom ye were called unto the fellowship of his Son Jesus Christ our Lord". (1 Corinthians 1:9)

The mystery of calling Gentiles unto salvation was not known in other ages, but it was revealed during the days of Apostle Paul, who wrote "That the Gentiles should be fellow-heirs, and of the same body, and partakers of his promise in Christ by the gospel". Paul preached unsearchable riches in Christ "And to make all men see what is the fellowship of the mystery, which from the beginning of the world hath been hid in God, who created all things by Jesus Christ" (Ephesians 3:9)

John testified about Lord Jesus Christ, whom he has seen physically as follows:

"That which we have seen and heard declare we unto you, that ye also may have fellowship with us: and truly our fellowship is with the Father, and with his Son Jesus Christ" (1 John 1:3)

Jesus is the Lord. Believe in Him and receive everlasting life.

OCTOBER DEVOTIONALS

DAY 1 MAN AT HIS BEST IS VANITY

In the presence of Martha, Mary, and the Jews, who were weeping and comforting the bereaved family, Jesus commanded to remove the stone, which was laid over the cave, where the dead body of Lazarus was laid to rest for four days then. Martha looked at Lord Jesus and said to Him "Lord, by this time he stinketh: for he hath been [dead] four days".

This was the same Martha, who said to Jesus earlier that she believed in Christ that He was the Son of God, who was to come into the world, as prophesied in the Old Testament. This was the same Martha, who said to Jesus that He was the resurrection and life, and later ran to her home to tell Mary that the Lord was coming to Bethany.

Now, when Jesus commanded that the stone covering the grave of Lazarus be removed she says "Lord, by this time he stinketh: for he hath been [dead] four days".

Speaking about man, his length of days on this earth, and his riches, Psalmist says:

"Behold, thou hast made my days [as] an handbreadth; and mine age [is] as nothing before thee: verily every man at his best state [is] altogether vanity. Selah" Psalm 39:5

If only God were to punish us according to the measure of our sins, we would not have deserved forgiveness or be able to stand before God. However,

"...God so loved the world, that he gave his only begotten Son, that whosoever believeth in him should not perish, but have everlasting life." John 3:16

Lord Jesus Christ paid price for our sins, made us righteous and justified. There is no condemnation to those who believe in Him.

DAY 2 THE BLESSED HOPE

Jesus admonishes Martha reminding her that if she believed in Him she will see the glory of God. Then, they took away the stone from the place where Lazarus was laid to rest. Then Jesus lifted up His eyes and prayed to the Father. In His prayer Jesus thanked the Father for hearing His prayer and said that the Father always hears Him. He prayed so in order that those who stood by Him may believe that the Father sent Him.

Jesus, after praying, cried out with a loud voice "Lazarus come forth". Notice Jesus called the dead man by his name; else, perhaps many dead would have come forth. The voice of Jesus was so powerful that the dead Lazarus rose to life and came forth. Another very noticeable fact is that the hand and foot of Lazarus were still bound with grave-clothes, and his face was bound with a napkin.

Comparison with the rising of the Lord Jesus Christ Himself, much later, when His hour was come, would show that the napkin that was bound on the face of Jesus was laid aside nicely folded, indicating that He Himself unloosened His bindings, and then folded the napkin that was bound on his head, and placed it at the side where His head was laid.

There was no assistance required for unloosening the wrap around the dead body of Jesus in the tomb. The tomb was covered with a stone, which was sealed and Jews made sure that no one stole His body. There was no scope of spreading false rumors that He was not raised from the dead, and yet there are many, in some circles, in the present generation, spreading false rumors that He did not die on the cross, nor did He rise from the dead. Indeed, Jesus died according to Scriptures, and there is evidence secular history as well. He appeared before many men, at different intervals, for forty days after His resurrection and before His ascension into heaven. He showed nail marks on his hands and feet to Thomas. He was the first-fruits.

Lord Jesus Christ commanded that Lazarus be unbound of the grave-clothes and the napkin that he may go. Thus, Lazarus was raised to life only to die again later because he was mortal, but Lord Jesus Christ was the Son of God, in the form of man, and therefore, His body did not see corruption in the grave and He rose in glorified body, which could pass closed doors, eat fish, appear and disappear at His will instantly at desired place.

It is the blessed hope of all believers in Christ that the dead will rise and receive glorified bodies, instantly, and those who are alive will follow them in similar glorified bodies, transformed at the twinkling of an eye, when they are ‘caught up’ at the coming of Lord Jesus again. (Cf. 1 Thessalonians 4:16-17, and 1 Corinthians 15:52)

DAY 3 CAN GOD BE CONFINED TO A CERTAIN PLACE?

Recounting the worship of idols, and sacrifices of beasts and human bodies to them by the descendants of Patriarchs, whom Stephen refers as 'your fathers', he says that they carried the Tabernacle on their way to the Promised Land, but had developed an idea of confining God to a place and temple.

When Solomon built the temple and some of the elements of the Tabernacle were placed in it, the children of Israel thought that God can be confined to a place. Stephen was exposing their utter misunderstanding of God when they blamed him that he was speaking against their holy place and the commandments of Moses. They had alleged that he was trying to break the commandments of Moses and teaching people to break them.

Stephen exposed their folly. The folly was that they gave their devotion to the host of heaven and offered sacrifices with delight to the idols.

In Acts 7:49 Stephen says that they took up tabernacle of Moloch, a sun-god, and Remphan, a moon or star-god, and worshipped them. He says, that after worshipping such idols they thought that the living God can also be confined to a place or in a temple. That was their understanding after Solomon built the temple.

The offering of the worship in the Tabernacle and building of Solomon's temple was in the plan of God, and He wanted the children of Israel to obey and keep his commandments.

Yet, their understanding that God can be confined to a place or in a temple was in error. Stephen, therefore, questions them if it was possible to confine God to a temple built with hands! The LORD said that Heaven was his throne and earth was his footstool and who could make him dwell in a place like Temple.

Thus saith the LORD, The heaven is my throne, and the earth is my footstool: where is the house that ye build unto me? and where is the place of my rest? (Isaiah 66:1)

Heaven is my throne, and earth is my footstool: what house will ye build me? saith the Lord: or what is the place of my rest? (Acts 7:49)

Stephen's point in defense against their false allegations was that they did not have perfect understanding about God and the temple. He defends himself that he never said that he would destroy the temple. He never spoke blasphemous words against the holy place or the Law of Moses. Peradventure even if he spoke such words as they alleged him of, he was not in error because their fathers were once idol-worshippers.

The elders and scribes lodged false allegations against Stephen that he said Jesus of Nazareth would destroy their holy place and change their customs which they derived from Moses. Stephen was innocent; and, therefore, he turned his defense into lay charge against them. He spoke boldly charging them that were stiff-necked and persecuted their fathers.

DAY 4 GOD WILL NOT LEAVE US IN LOW PROFILE

"Blessed is that man that maketh the LORD his trust, and respecteth not the proud, nor such as turn aside to lies". (Psalms 40:4)

Joseph became an important figure in Potiphar's house. Joseph was well built and handsome. Potiphar's wife lured him but Joseph flew from that wicked act. Potiphar's wife acted as if Joseph tried to seduce her, and so Potiphar put him in prison.

There were to cup bearers of Potiphar also in prison. Joseph had dreams which he interpreted saying that they will be restored to their old positions. He requested one of the cup bearers to remember him before Potiphar, when he is restored, but the cup bearer forgot him.

It was after two full years that Pharaoh's chief cup bearer remembered Joseph when Pharaoh had two dreams and desired someone interpret his dreams.

Pharaoh was very much disturbed after seeing these two dreams one after another. In one of the dreams he saw seven sleek and fat cows grazed on the banks of Nile and there came out of the Nile seven other cows ugly and gaunt and ate up the seven sleek and fat cows. In the next dream he saw seven heads of grain healthy and good were growing good and then sprouted other seven thin heads of grain, which swallowed up seven healthy heads of grain.

Not a single magician or wise man in the land could interpret the dreams Pharaoh had. This was the time when the chief cup bearer remembered Joseph, who was with him in the prison, and interpreted for him his dream that came true and was restored to his position as chief cup bearer.

The chief cup bearer told Pharaoh about Joseph's interpretations of his dream that came true. Pharaoh was delighted to know about Joseph and he immediately called for him. Joseph was brought from the dungeon and when he had shaved and changed clothes he was presented before Pharaoh. He explained to Joseph the dreams he had and asked him to interpret.

Joseph gave the preeminence to God and said that it was not through his own capability that he interpreted the dreams but by God's help. He also acknowledged that he cannot do anything himself without God's help. He said it was God who will interpret the dreams for him.

After hearing from Pharaoh his dreams, Joseph with the help of God, interpreted the dreams to Pharaoh, and told him that the two dreams are one and the same.

God revealed that there will be seven years of abundance in Egypt and then will follow seven years of famine. Pharaoh was very much pleased with Joseph's interpretations of the dreams and, therefore, made him in charge of the land of Egypt. Joseph managed everything well with the help of God. He filled the garners with food during the seven years of abundance to meet with the needs of people during the seven years of famine. (Genesis 39:7-)

When we offer ourselves in to the hands of God, give preeminence to God, and allow Him to lead us He will elevate us. Though at present it may appear that we are in bad position, yet it should be noted that it is God who puts down one and it is He who elevates a person.

There is certainly hope that our living God will not leave us in a low profile for a long time, but elevate us in due season, and according to his plan. Joseph was not left behind in prison, but he was not only released from prison, but he was made ruler in Egypt.

"Humble yourselves therefore under the mighty hand of God, that he may exalt you in due time: Casting all your care upon him; for he careth for you." (1 Peter 5:6-7)

DAY 5 THE FEAST OF TRUMPETS

"The Feast of the Trumpets" is the fifth feast of the "Feasts of the LORD" described in Leviticus Chapter 23. This feast is celebrated on the first day of the seventh month. After redeeming the children of Israel from the bondage of slavery under Pharaoh the LORD said to the children of Israel through Moses, his servant, that they should celebrate seven feasts in remembrance of how God redeemed them with his "outstretched arm" from the bondage.

These feasts were to be celebrated in two different periods of Hebrew Calendar year when they come into the Promised Land.

The first festival of the seventh month is the "Feast of Trumpets" which was celebrated on the first day of the seventh month, the second feast of the seventh month is "The feast of Day of Atonement" which was celebrated on the 10th day of seventh month, and the third feast of the seventh month is "The Feast of Tabernacles" which was celebrated on the 15th day of the seventh month.

The "Feast of the Trumpets" was not only a memorial to remember the mighty power of God but also shows the future events. The "Feast of Trumpets" calls us for Repentance that results in Redemption which gives us the privilege of Rejoicing. These future events include "Rapture" of the Church, "Jacob's Trouble" and the opening of the Books (Revelation 20:12) and opening of the Gates (Revelation chapter 21 and Revelation 22:14).

"And the LORD spake unto Moses, saying, Speak unto the children of Israel, saying, In the seventh month, in the first day of the month, shall ye have a sabbath, a memorial of blowing of trumpets, an holy convocation. Ye shall do no servile work therein: but ye shall offer an offering made by fire unto the LORD". (Leviticus 23:23-25)

Did you ever wonder how God arranged the movements of two and half million children of Israel when they were journeying from Egypt to Canaan in the wilderness, treading rough roads, mountains, and be triumphant in the wars against their enemies en-route and amidst dangerous animals? It was by the usage of Trumpets that the children of Israel gathered at designated places and gave obedience to their leaders.

The horn of ram that was caught in the thicket when Abraham was trying to offer Isaac as sacrifice was used as Trumpet. Later the children of Israel developed on that and used for specific purposes ordered by God. The usage of trumpets was like calling God's help. God asked Joshua to use trumpets to bring down Jericho and its walls fell down with the blowing of trumpets (Joshua 6:20)

"And the LORD shall be seen over them, and his arrow shall go forth as the lightning: and the Lord GOD shall blow the trumpet, and shall go with whirlwinds of the south". (Zechariah 9:14)

New Testament believer is member of the Church, which is

the bride of Christ, will be with the Lord Jesus Christ for ever and ever.

"For the Lord himself shall descend from heaven with a shout, with the voice of the archangel, and with the trump of God: and the dead in Christ shall rise first: Then we which are alive and remain shall be caught up together with them in the clouds, to meet the Lord in the air: and so shall we ever be with the Lord. 1 Thessalonians 4:16, 17

DAY 6 LAW AND GRACE

PAUL EXPLAINS TO GALATIANS

Paul explains to Galatians, just as a matured man explaining to children that all those who believe that law can save them are like those, who are of 'bondwoman' and all those who believe in the 'grace' of Jesus are like those, who are of free woman. He quotes from Old Testament the things that have happened in *Abram*'s life as described in Genesis 16th Chapter. *Sarai* sent her handmaid, Hagar to sleep with Abram, and a son was born. It was legalism on the part of *Sarai* and *Abram* a method that finds a way out for them. Later a son was born to **Abraham** and his wife **Sarah** as a consequence of the promise of God to them.

This son of the promise of God was of faith in God and His grace. The son, who was born to Hagar, was of the flesh, and the son born of promise to Sarai, was blessed. The posterity of bondwoman is still under bondage of Mosaic Law and the posterity of the free woman, who is supposed to be free from the bondage of Mosaic Law, have unfortunately, embraced the law and works as their way for salvation, rejected Messiah as their Savior, and is still under the bondage of law. Paul allegorizes these two to 'Agar', which is in Mount Sinai that answers to Jerusalem, which is on this earth. Paul desires that everyone should embrace the belief that it is by 'grace' of God that saves a man.

Paul allegorizes this to the Jerusalem, which is above all, that consists of the posterity of Isaac, born of **Sarah** and that 'grace' alone saves a person. The legalists still insist that it is right to be under the law and keep the law to be saved. Such legalism will lead to the belief that there is no justification by the grace of God, but their own works will lead them to have eternal life.

A question arises in the minds of those, who are confused about law and how it differs from 'grace' with regard to salvation that is available to all of us through Jesus. The question that could be considered is that why God gave law in the first place, and then asked us not to subject ourselves to law but be under 'grace'

Apostle Paul writes that the law is not against the promises of God, but it was given in order that man may understand that the transgressions he committed cannot be forgiven by law. Law points out the guilt of a person and shows why he should not be punished under law for violating it.. Under the law priest had to offer sacrifice first and then offer a sacrifice for the person, who is guilty.

If law could make a person righteous, truly righteousness should have been by law, but the Scripture has concluded every one as having come short of the glory of God and that everyone is sinful. The promise by faith of Lord Jesus Christ was made available only to those who believe in the efficacy of his blood and his death upon the cross for our sake. He bore our sins, died for our sake. He was buried and was raised from the dead.

The law was our schoolmaster in order to teach us the way unto Jesus, who is the only mediator, and that no one else can save a person, nor can any other price or works or law associated with works can save a person from eternal condemnation. We can be justified only by faith in him.

After Jesus had become propitiation for us, it is not required of us to do what is to be done under the law in order to have salvation; but faith in him alone is enough; and that is to say that we are no longer under the schoolmaster. As many as have believed and accepted Jesus Christ as personal Savior and Lord, have put on Christ, irrespective of whether they are Jews or Greeks, bonded or free, or male or female. All those, who are saved with the precious blood of Jesus Christ are one in him and all such saved persons belong to him and are Abraham's seed by faith and have inherited the promises.

DAY 7 PAUL ADMONISHES GALATIANS

Paul's feels as if he was under the travail of child birth to explain to Galatians the difference between law and grace, and how hard it is to be under law rather than accept 'grace' alone as the way for salvation. He calls them, now, 'my little children', and tries to explain to them about the implications in believing that law and works only would save them.

Galatians were under the erroneous belief that law and works only can save them. They desired to take pride in a list of rules they prescribed for them and as they keep the rules they would consider them as perfect.

That, in other words, renders a notion that man can earn his own salvation by keeping a set of rules, like being good and doing good etc.

These things help men to be good men but would not secure salvation that is available free of cost as a result of belief in the works of Jesus, the Son of God, did for men. He came down into this world to redeem us from the bondage of sin, and, therefore, took upon himself, our transgressions and died for our sake.

The fruits of the Holy Spirit are love, joy, peace, longsuffering, gentleness, goodness, faith, Meekness, temperance. A saved man will have in him the Spirit of God and will have the fruits of the Holy Spirit. However, possession of these good qualities without accepting Jesus as 'Lord' will not make us a man eligible to have eternal life. The only way to have eternal life is to believe in the efficacy of the blood of Jesus Christ and accept the fact that he died in our stead on the cross.

Admonishing Galatians time and again, Apostle Paul continues to emphasize on the fact that there is salvation only in Jesus through faith by grace and not by law and works associated with it.

Getting entangled with law and with the thought that they need to do something to be saved, is tantamount to be under the yoke of bondage, he says. About, circumcision, he condemns it and says that if anyone is of the belief that circumcision is necessary for salvation or for justification, the obsession of such thought will not profit them and Christ and his blood is of nothing to them.

Everyone, who is circumcised, becomes debtor to the whole law and Christ and his sacrifice has nothing for him. We are reckoned as righteous only by faith in Jesus and by his grace. Neither circumcision nor un-circumcision avails anything to a believer in Christ.

Walking in the Spirit and hatred of lust of the flesh are necessary on the part of a believer to lead a holy life. One great truth a believer has to understand is that flesh lusts against the Spirit and the Spirit against the flesh and these are contrary to each other. If we are of the Spirit and are led by the Spirit we are not under the law and would not yield to the desires of the flesh.

After having known of the love of God through His one only begotten son, Jesus, why would we turn yet unto beggarly elements like observing the days, months, times and years, and be subject again to be under the bondage of the law? When the price for our sin and redemption is already paid for, why would we turn again to work for our salvation by ourselves? Salvation is available free of cost; the price is already paid for. All that is needed on the part of sinner is to believe that Jesus paid the price of his sin on the cross, and that he needs to believe in his/her heart this fact and accept him as his/her personal Savior.

DAY 8 PAUL BLESSES

Apostle Paul blesses those, who do not voluntarily subject themselves to be under the yoke of law, but accept Christ's death upon the cross. He says fulfilling the law of Christ is more important than that of the Old Testament laws. No one should boast of himself nor glory himself/herself, but everyone should glorify Lord Jesus Christ, whose marks were borne by not only Apostle Paul but all those, who realize the efficacy of the blood of Lord Jesus Christ. Are Law and Works necessary for salvation?

Speaking of law and grace and the firm belief of Jews that law plus works are essential for their salvation rather than depending on pure mercy of God by grace through faith, another point that we could meditate is as to why God did not have his own people, Jews, realize this so quickly that pure grace from God is alone sufficient for their salvation.

There is enough reason, as we understand, that God not only wanted his own people, Jews, to have their salvation, but also Gentiles to enjoy that privilege of calling him as 'Abba, Father'.

Apostle Paul wonders if God had cast away his people; but then he immediately reaffirms that it was not so, because he was also of the seed of Abraham, of the tribe of Benjamin. God did not cast away his people, whom he foreknew.

Even when Elias was taking pride in himself that he was alone available to intercede on behalf of Israel, God said to him, that he had reserved seven thousand men unto him, who could intercede on behalf of Israel. If the salvation, therefore, is by 'grace', then it is not by 'works'.

What then happened exactly that the attitude and belief of Jews has not changed yet? Yes, it is because God blinded their eyes and gave them spiritual slumber, that they should not see and that they may not have ears for hearing unto this day. Have Israel stumbled that they should fall then?

Apostle Paul himself answers these questions (Romans 11th Chapter) that God did not blind them or made them deaf because they were stumbling blocks or it was because they have stumbled, but because of the desire God had that everyone in the world, irrespective of Jews or Gentiles be saved and have eternal life.

Apostle Paul questions as to who has known the mind of Lord, who has been his counselor. It is obvious that God's thoughts are higher than ours and His ways are un-understandable to us. In the book of Hosea the pathetic condition of Israel is described. In this book it is seen that Israel, who had been blessed and to whom were the blessings and covenants given, continually fell from the presence of the Lord. In the sight of the Lord, who asked Hosea to marry a prostitute, Israel was similar to Prostitute, dishonest with her infidelity.

God, who was like husband to them had to see her deviation from the honesty and loyalty, had to chastise them time and again.

The Lord goes on to say that they are not his people, and he is not their God. He was like a frustrated husband trying to bring them to the path of salvation, yet they erred time and again. This was the reason, why God had to extend salvation to the Gentiles, thus making Jews and Gentiles one in Christ.

It was not a mystery that the Gentiles should be saved but one mystery was certainly there that God would form Church consisting of Jews and Gentiles, and that Church is above Jews and Gentiles. This purpose was hidden in God until it was revealed to us in Ephesians 2nd Chapter.

The Church is the body of Christ. In this Church are no differences as to who is Jew and who is Gentile, but everyone has similar status. In this Church is seen no more distinction of earthly differences of race, ethnicity, clan, color, and nationality. It is the blood of Jesus that saves a man from being condemned to death and eternal destruction. It is the water that Jesus gives that becomes living water for the sinner. It is the life that Jesus gives to sinner that becomes eternal life.

DAY 9 PAUL WARNS GENTILES

More than anyone taking of airs of his belonging to any clan the important fact that is to be borne in mind is that it is the grace of God that saves a man.

No man needs precious metals such as gold and silver to earn a place in new Jerusalem, but all that a man needs is to have simple faith in Jesus, the Son of God and make him Lord of his/her life. God wipes away their tears. There shall be no more death, no more sorrow, no more crying and no more pain. God shall give freely to all that thirst for such a life the fountain of life. He who overcomes the world and the temptations therein shall inherit the blessings from God and he shall be His son. Salvation to Gentiles

Apostle Paul explains in Romans 11th Chapter elaborately God's provisions and His plan for the salvation of Gentiles. He writes that it was not because of Israel's stumbling or because they were stumbling blocks to anybody that their eyes were blinded; that their ears were hard on hearing.

They fell short of understanding Messiah, and believed that they need to do something for their salvation. They always insisted that because God had done some good for them they also need to do some good for God as recompense. They think that they owe to God some obligation. It is because of their misunderstanding, and rejection of Jesus as their Messiah that salvation is come unto the Gentiles.

Psalmist writes..."What shall I render unto the LORD for all his benefits toward me? I will take the cup of salvation, and call upon the name of the LORD. Psalms 116:12-13".

The Lord says..."If I were hungry, I would not tell thee: for the world is mine, and the fulness thereof. Will I eat the flesh of bulls, or drink the blood of goats? Psalms 50:12-13

Paul warns Gentiles that they are like grafted wild olive tree in the places, where the branches of the natural branches were broken off. The Gentiles are partakers of the root and fatness of the natural olive tree. Therefore, he says, Gentiles should not be of high-minded, but fear.

The branches of the natural olive tree were broken off by God himself, because of their unbelief, and the Gentiles, who were like wild olive trees have, now, the sap and blessings from the root of the natural olive tree.

If Gentiles were to be high-minded and take pride in themselves or their own merits, God will not hesitate to chastise them. If God did not spare the natural branches of the olive tree would he tolerate the grafted olive tree; never! Did God spare Jews from chastisement?

The warning Apostle Paul gave to Gentiles in Romans 11th Chapter does not mean that salvation would be lost, but of the severity of the chastisement that they face at God's hands in cases where they do not realize the goodness of God.

He quotes the chastisement that the Jews suffered at the hands of the Almighty God for the thought that they had that their merits would save them. Jews have neither recognized the Son of God, when he came down to this earth, as their Messiah, nor did they give cognizance to the efficacy of the blood of Jesus, who bore not only their sins but of the whole world. The Israel would not remain in the present state of their blindness of the love of Jesus, but soon they would come out from it and see clearly who their Savior was.

This will not happen until the fullness of the Gentiles is come in. The Scriptures are clear that all Israel shall be saved. Messiah will turn away from them their ungodliness because of the covenant God made with the Patriarchs.

Whoever accepts Jesus as his/her personal Savior, will have eternal life. God has concluded all Israel in unbelief and it is time now for Gentiles to accept Jesus as their personal Savior.

DAY 10 SIN CAN NOT HAVE DOMINION

All the Saved are equal before God

Jesus Christ has abolished separation once and for all, and gave Gentiles the privilege of being equal to be with Jews. The Jews and Gentiles, who believed Jesus as their Savior, are part of the Church, which does not recognize either Jews or Gentiles as separate entities. Jesus fulfilled the law and he has abolished in the 'flesh the enmity, even the law of commandments contained in ordinances'. The reconciliation with God and man; and with Jews and Gentiles is achieved through the shed blood of Jesus. The cleansing of sins has resulted in crucifixion of our old man in us and putting on new man.

"Knowing this, that our old man is crucified with him, that the body of sin might be destroyed, that henceforth we should not serve sin" (Romans 6:6)

"And that ye put on the new man, which after God is created in righteousness and true holiness". (Ephesians 4:24)

One of the reasons why Jews had a barrier between them and the Gentiles was because they believed that the Gentiles did not keep the law. Jews treated the Gentiles with contempt that they were not the children of Jacob (Israel). Jesus is the way, the truth and the life and we have access to the Father through His one and only begotten Son, Jesus Christ, who is our mediator, and by the Spirit. Therefore, we are no longer 'strangers and foreigners but fellow citizens with the saints and of the household of God'.

Jesus says 'Come unto me, all ye that labour and are heavy laden, and I will give you rest'. He said that children should not be forbidden to come unto him. By making Jews and Gentiles as one body and by breaking the 'middle wall of partition' he made peace between God and man, Jews and Gentiles. That is the reconciliation.

Jesus made peace through his blood that was shed on the cross so as to reconcile all things unto himself, irrespective of their belonging to earth or to heaven. Therefore, everything belongs to God, who has reconciled us to Himself by Jesus Christ. In order that our trespasses may not be imputed to us, God has given us the ministry of reconciliation and he has committed unto us the word of reconciliation. God was in Christ when He was reconciling us unto Himself.

[References: Matthew 11:28, Matthew 19:14, 2 Corinthians 5:18 and 19, Colossians 1:20, Ephesians 2:14-19]

Apostle Paul emphasizes (in Romans 6th chapter) that sin shall not have dominion over born-again child because he/she is not under the law, but under grace. Those who seek to do good works and earn salvation by their own works do nullify the importance of blood of Jesus Christ.

The blood of Jesus Christ that cleanses the sin has no value for them. They diligently keep doing good works in order to receive salvation neglecting the repeated emphasis from the Lord Jesus Christ that there is eternal life only in and through him. The blood of Jesus shed on the cross of Calvary can only save a person. This is the only way to receive eternal life. Salvation is available to all those who go to him and accept him as the Lord.

Now, here is the question:

After having been delivered from the bondage of sin by grace through faith should a child of God keep sinning because he is under the grace but not under law?

Paul very firmly says, “God forbid”. Never should a child of God return to sin and lose blessings from God. Salvation is not lost for those who are saved in the blood of Jesus Christ; however, the Scripture does not endorse repeated sinning. God will surely chide and chastise the one that falls repeatedly into sin and seeks grace time and again.

Should we not consider the fact that if we yield to sin we are servants to sin; and sin becomes our master? We are under grace and we should remain servants to our Lord and be obedient to put on Christ as written in Ephesians 4:24 and live righteous life.

We were, once servants of sin; but after accepting Jesus as our master, we have become servants of righteousness. We should bear fruit unto the Lord by leading a life of holiness and have assurance that there is everlasting life for us in eternity. The law has concluded all of us under sin, but the gift of God is eternal life through Lord Jesus Christ.

DAY 11 ANOTHER GOSPEL

Apostle Paul writes about 'another gospel' in Galatians 1st Chapter. What this 'another Gospel' is?

'Gospel' means good news. Gospel of Jesus Christ means good news of Jesus Christ. There is another gospel about which Apostle Paul writes in Galatians 1:6 and 7

"I marvel that ye are so soon removed from him that called you into the grace of Christ unto another gospel: Which is not another; but there be some that trouble you, and would pervert the gospel of Christ". (Galatians 1:6-7)

This 'another gospel' dispels the efficacy of the blood of Jesus Christ and gives importance to law and works associated with it. This gospel seeks to add works to faith in Christ. It shows that mere faith in Jesus is not enough to be saved but good works need to be done. While good works follow salvation, they are not conditional for receiving salvation.

Paul writes to the Church in Thessalonica that when they received the word of God, which they heard it from him, they received it not as the word of men, but as the truth from the word of God. He says that the truth of the Gospel will lead them to repent of their sins and help them to believe in Jesus Christ. (1 Thessalonians 2:13)

In 1 Corinthians 15th Chapter Paul speaks of Resurrection of Jesus Christ and our resurrection. This is good news for those who hope in Jesus Christ and believe that he is the savior. This gospel will benefit only those who receive it and believe in it. If a sinner does not believe in the Gospel of Jesus Christ and about his resurrection, the Gospel is of no use to him even though he repents of his sin. The sinner needs to confess by his mouth that Jesus Christ is the Lord, and believe in his heart that God raised him from the dead. Only this belief will save him.

"That if thou shalt confess with thy mouth the Lord Jesus, and shalt believe in thine heart that God hath raised him from the dead, thou shalt be saved". (Romans 10:9)

Paul writes that he delivered good news that which he first received and believed. He wrote that Christ died for our sins and rose from the dead according to Scriptures.

"For I delivered unto you first of all that which I also received, how that Christ died for our sins according to the scriptures; And that he was buried, and that he rose again the third day according to the scriptures: (1 Corinthians 15:3-4).

This is the good news and there is no other way for salvation than to believe in Jesus as personal Savior. The death of Jesus upon the cross only was the way to redeem us from our sins. In his resurrection we have the great news that there is none who rose from the dead, the way the Lord Jesus was raised.

Any other gospel preached to reduce or nullify the efficacy of the blood of Lord Jesus Christ is 'another gospel'. Such gospel is not the true gospel but perversion of 'Gospel'. Apostle Paul warns us to be careful of such false preaching.

DAY 12 THE MESSAGE OF CROSS

Apostle Paul writes that the message of the cross of Christ is foolishness to those, who are perishing, but to those who are saved it is the power of God.

When he came to know that there were contentions and divisions among the followers of Christ, and some of them identifying themselves as belonging to Apollos, and some to Cephas, and some to Christ, he questions them if Christ was divided? He further questions them if he (Paul) was crucified for them.

To the Jews the message of cross was not acceptable because they did not believe that Jesus bore our sins on the cross; rather they wanted to see signs and proofs. To the Greeks, who believed in philosophy and wisdom of this world, the message of cross was foolishness.

Paul's main motto was to preach the gospel of Jesus, "Who gave himself for our sins, that he might deliver us from this present evil world, according to the will of God and our Father" (Galatians 1:4) rather than baptizing.

He laid emphasis on preaching 'Christ curried' rather than usage of clever and attractive words, luring men into false confidence, and false promises of good health, or enough wealth, or guaranteed prosperous life.

Any other type of preaching without showing the truth of the cross where the Son of God shed his precious blood will be of no effect. Temporary assuage may be achieved by preaching resting on false promises, but sooner or later such preaching would be denounced.

God destroys the wise men of this world that treat the message of cross with contempt. Everything in this world is transient and temporary. What lasts is the eternal life that can be had only by faith in Jesus, who has paid price for our salvation. It is the gift of God and cannot be purchased with any amount of wealth of this world. (1 Corinthians 1:17-23) Who was last Adam?

Apostle Paul refers to two representatives of all humans in 1 Corinthians 15:45 "And so it is written, The first man Adam was made a living soul; the last Adam was made a quickening spirit". Lord Jesus was fully man and fully divine. Here in this verse, Paul refers to the human form of Jesus and calls him as the last Adam. The first man on this earth, Adam, sinned and brought condemnation as heritage for everyone.

Condemnation is severe reproof, or accusation. In Adam everyone is condemned. Added to that, we all commit sins. Romans 3:23 says we all have sinned and come short of the glory of God. Romans 6:23 says that 'the wages of sin is death; but the gift of God is eternal life through Jesus Christ our Lord'.

As we are all sinners, being the sons and daughters from Adam and Eve, who transgressed God's commandment, we deserved nothing but condemnation and judgment; but through the gift of grace that is given by Lord Jesus and having accepted this gift by faith in him, this condemnation and judgment are put away from us, and we are justified. By 'the offence of one judgment came upon all men to condemnation but the free gift is of many offences unto justification'. (Romans 5:18).

"There is therefore now no condemnation to them which are in Christ Jesus, who walk not after the flesh, but after the Spirit". Romans 8:1

The Scriptures say that if we say we have no sin, we not only deceive ourselves, but we make God a liar. Therefore, everyone should accept before God that he has sinned and ask for forgiveness. The forgiveness is free from God, and there is no need to pay silver or Gold. The price is already paid by Jesus Christ on the cross of Calvary.

DAY 13 WHO WE WERE?

The Bible points out as to who were we before accepting Lord Jesus as our personal savior, and who are we like after accepting Lord Jesus as our personal savior. Our sinful condition before we are born-again is shown in the Scriptures.

Bible says we were dead in trespasses and sins. Yes, we were dead; dead in trespasses; our trespasses were anathema to God; we were dead in sins our sinful nature was hated by God; but God loved us even when we were dead in trespasses, and even when we were in that sinful nature.

That is why he sent his only begotten son, Jesus into this world for our sake. Whoever accepts Jesus as his personal savior is saved from eternal damnation. Those who believe in Jesus Christ as their personal savior, there is the quickening of the spirit. They are called as 'born again'. They are redeemed from the bondage of sin. They saved unto eternal life.

There is one point we need to understand that 'dead in trespasses' does not mean that a man is fully dead in all respects to the extent that he cannot believe on Jesus, but it means that Satan has blinded man's beliefs and understanding to the extent that the Scriptural truth appears to him as foolishness.

When Jesus said to Nicodemus, a ruler of the Jews that "...Verily, verily, I say unto thee, Except a man be born again, he cannot see the kingdom of God", Nicodemus questioned Jesus as to what exactly the word 'born-again' means. He asked Jesus if a man should enter the womb of his mother again to be 'born-again'.

Then, Jesus answered, "Verily, verily, I say unto thee, Except a man be born of water and of the Spirit, he cannot enter into the kingdom of God" (John 3:3-5)

Sin held us as slaves; it made us blind to the truth of the Gospel of Jesus Christ; it brought us under condemnation; it had us as aliens from the commonwealth of Israel; it made us strangers to the covenants of promise; it held us in a state of hopelessness; and it treated us a strangers and foreigners to the living God.

Even when we were in that situation God showed his love toward us.

I John 4:9-10 read:

"In this was manifested the love of God toward us, because that God sent his only begotten Son into the world, that we might live through him. Herein is love, not that we loved God, but that he loved us, and sent his Son to be the propitiation for our sins. "

God delivered us and made us servants of righteousness. We, who were the children of wrath are given the privilege of calling the living God, as 'Abba, Father'. He has given us the privilege to be called as sons of God. He has translated us into the Kingdom of His dear Son.

The only demand that God has placed on a sinner is to repent of his sins and call on Jesus to forgive his/her sins. Entire price for redemption from sinful life is paid for by Jesus on the cross. There is nothing that a sinner needs to do except believing in the blood of Jesus, who paid the price for our redemption already.

(References: Ephesians 2nd Chapter, 2 Cor. 4:3-4, Romans 6:17-18, John 3:19-20, Mark 2:17, Luke 15th Chapter, Col 1:13).

DAY 14 GOD KNOWS OUR WEAKNESS

"And the LORD God formed man of the dust of the ground, and breathed into his nostrils the breath of life; and man became a living soul". (Genesis 2:7)

God formed our bodies with the dust of the ground. When he created the first man, on this earth he breathed his life into the nostrils of the man and the man (Adam) became a living soul. The living soul that God created was in the image of God.

After man had committed sin he lost that image of God, and 'death reigned from Adam to Moses even over that had not sinned after the similitude of Adam's transgression'. By the offence of one many came under the penalty of death, but by the gift of God that is 'grace' many have become eligible to receive eternal life.

It was by one, (Adam), who sinned that death came to reign on man, and it is by the ONE (Jesus), that the gift of God is available for all sinners. All those who accept that the Son of God, Jesus, died for his/her sins, and accept him as the 'Lord' of one's life are saved from damnation. It is then that the soul dead in trespasses is redeemed; it is then that the soul is delivered from suffering the wrath of God.

The soul that does not repent of his/her sins will be cast into lake of fire, by God, after the 'Great white throne judgment', which is the final judgment.

As and when our earthly house of this tabernacle gets dissolved we gain a building of God, the house not made with hands, but that which would be eternal in heavens.

We groan in this body desiring to be clothed upon; we suffer diseases because our earthly bodies are made of dust. But, there will come a day when this body made of dust returns to dust, but the sprit ascends. King Solomon said… "Then shall the dust return to the earth as it was: and the spirit shall return unto God who gave it". (Ecclesiastes 12:7)

Our groaning will end when we rise up with our glorified bodies. We rejoice in the Lord because we have a soul that does not perish, but will be with the Lord in eternity.

Apostle Paul wrote… "In a moment, in the twinkling of an eye, at the last trump: for the trumpet shall sound, and the dead shall be raised incorruptible, and we shall be changed. For this corruptible must put on incorruption, and this mortal must put on immortality". (1 Corinthians" 15:52-53)

"For the Lord himself shall descend from heaven with a shout, with the voice of the archangel, and with the trump of God: and the dead in Christ shall rise first" (1 Thessalonians 4:16)

It is so comforting to know that God forgives our sins, no matter how serious they were, provided we repent of our sins and seek forgiveness. He is loving and compassionate.

Psalmist writes: "For he knoweth our frame; he remembereth that we are dust". (Psalms 103:14) Jesus broke down the middle wall of partition

Jesus, the Son of God, is our peace; he has broken down the middle wall of partition between us and the Father. He has abolished in his flesh the enmity that had us captive under the law of commandments contained in ordinances. He has done this to make us new, and did this for our sake to help us have peace with the Father. He preached peace to us, who were far off and also to those who were near. Through Jesus we have now access by one Spirit unto the Father. This is the reason why we are longer strangers and foreigners, but we are now fellow-citizens with saints, and we are the members of His house.

Why then should we serve the law? The law was added because of transgressions until 'the seed should come to whom the promise was made. Jesus, having become the mediator did not become lower in stature nor in status, and he is not a mediator of one, but God is one.

There is one God, and the mediator between the Father and us is the man Christ Jesus, who received an excellent ministry of a better covenant that was established on better promises. He redeemed us from the transgressions of the first testament in order that we, who are called, 'might receive the promise of eternal inheritance'. The blood of Jesus shed upon the cross speaks better things than that of Abel, who brought of the firstlings of his flock and its fat, which was pleasing to God.

The two commandments that Jesus gave to New Testament believers have in them the essence of all the Ten Commandments.

The two commandments the Jesus gave are: 'And thou shalt love the Lord thy God with all thy heart, and with all thy soul, and with all thy mind, and with all thy strength: this is the first commandment. And the second is like, namely this, Thou shalt love thy neighbour as thyself. There is none other commandment greater than these' Mark 12:30-31

(Ref: Gen 4:4, Galatians 3rd Ch. 1 Timothy 2:5, Hebrews 8, 9 and 10th Chapters)

DAY 15 CAN MAN BE SAVED BY OWN EFFORTS

When someone insists on keeping the law in order to obtain salvation and then be counted as righteous before God, it is no doubt, tantamount to making his/she own efforts to achieve eternal life without the help from God. As a consequence of his/her own efforts he/she tries to be perfect in all respects. It would then call for introspection to see if the person is indeed keeping all the provisions of the law that are to be kept mandatorily as laid down by God.

The introspection would bring conviction that even in keeping the law meticulously the law finds him guilty on one count or the other. The only recourse left for man is to take refuge in the 'grace' of God given abundantly to us, through His only begotten Son Jesus Christ. As written in Romans 2 Chapter, those without the law shall perish without law, and those that have sinned in the law will become liable for judgment under the law.

Inasmuch as the law was given by God through Moses, Gentiles are reckoned as having no law, and therefore, if they try to obey the law meticulously, they are making the law unto themselves; the law that was not given by God. They accuse and excuse one another according to their own law.

As for Jews the Scripture calls them 'blind' who guide the 'blind', a light of them who are in 'darkness', an instructor of the 'foolish', a teacher of 'babes', Scriptures asks Jews, who teach others about law, as to why they do not teach unto themselves the law and strict provision therein? If they are true to their teaching, then are they not stealing, while teaching not to steal? Why do they commit adultery? Bible is very strict on them that they being teachers of the law, they break the law and commit idolatry, resulting in blasphemy of God among the Gentiles. Circumcision profits only if the law is kept in perfect sense, but if one of the provisions of the law is broken, circumcision is tantamount to un-circumcision.

The punishments under law are very severe. Neither Jew nor Gentile can have redemption from their sins, if they rely on keeping the law and be justified. God invites everyone to accept 'grace' available through Jesus Christ, the only begotten Son of God and receive salvation. (Romans 2:12-29)

DAY 16 REDEMPTION AND JUSTIFICATION

REDEMPTION

Redemption, in the context of New Testament doctrine, is getting something back for the price paid; in other words, setting forth a sinner free from the bondage of sin with the price paid by Jesus Christ on the cross. It is to deliver by paying price.

There are three things that take place in the process of redemption. It is buying something that was under bondage. It was setting free from the bondage and it is freeing from that bondage. This is what exactly what Christ did on the cross on behalf of sinner.

Every man is under the bondage of sin from the time he is born in the womb of his mother. Scripture says, there is no one righteous, and anyone who does not accept this fact is making the writer of the Scripture a liar -- '1 John 1:10 If we say that we have not sinned, we make him a liar, and his word is not in us.'

The man under the bondage of sin needs deliverance. This is what Christ did on the cross by dying in the stead of sinner taking upon himself the sins of the sinner fulfilling the law. Every man, who is freed from the bondage needs to be delivered just as a product or animal is taken out of the market place and freed.

This is what Jesus did by freeing from the bondage of sin, and delivering us from the penalty of sin, which is death. Our bodies perish and we rise in glory with glorified bodies. While the bodies still lay in the grave and perish, the soul of a believer is eternally present with the Lord Jesus Christ right from the movement is gives up his earthly life.

Romans 7:13 Was then that which is good made death unto me? God forbid. But sin, that it might appear sin, working death in me by that which is good; that sin by the commandment might become exceeding sinful.

The law pointed out sin, but the grace delivered us from the bondage of sin. Accepting Jesus as the Lord and Savior will set a sinner free from the bondage of sin, and entitles him to have eternal life. What is Justification?

1 Corinthians 1:30 But of him are ye in Christ Jesus, who of God is made unto us wisdom, and righteousness, and sanctification, and redemption

JUSTIFICATION

Justification is the declaration that our Lord and Savior Jesus Christ makes before the Father about a sinner, who believes in Jesus Christ and accepts him as his personal Savior.

The sinner, who confesses him as the 'Lord' is justified by him as righteous because Christ has borne the sins of sinner on the cross of Calvary and made him righteous. The justification originates in and through the grace. It is by grace through faith in him that a sinner is saved.

No amount of good works can save a person, nor can justify him as righteous before God. Romans 3:24 Being justified freely by his grace through the redemption that is in Christ Jesus. It is judicial act that Jesus has performed on the cross. He paid the price for the redemption of sinner. He died in the stead of a sinner. That is how he justifies the sinner as righteous before the Father.

All that a sinner needs to do is to accept the fact that Jesus Christ has died on the cross in his stead and rose from the dead on the third day. It is by faith in Jesus as the redeemer that a sinner is saved and no charge is laid against him, irrespective of what gross sin he/she has committed.

Every sin, except blasphemy of Holy Spirit, is pardonable by God. Christ has established the law by taking upon himself the penalty of sin, which is death. Our Inheritance in heaven is incorruptible

Peter reveals a marvelous truth in 1 Peter 1st Chapter. Addressing to the strangers scattered throughout Pontus, Galatia, Cappadocia, Asia and Bithynia he calls on Elect by God the Father, and wishes them 'Grace'.

He says all those, whom he addressed, were begotten unto lively hope by the resurrection of Jesus Christ from the dead and to inherit incorruptible and undefiled rewards that do not fade away. These are reserved for them in heaven.

1 Peter 1:3-4 read...Blessed be the God and Father of our Lord Jesus Christ, which according to his abundant mercy hath begotten us again unto a lively hope by the resurrection of Jesus Christ from the dead, To an inheritance incorruptible, and undefiled, and that fadeth not away, reserved in heaven for you.

We read in 2 Timothy 3:16 that 'All scripture is given by

inspiration of God, and is profitable for doctrine, for reproof, for correction, for instruction in righteousness'.

Everyone, irrespective of his belonging to the clan of Jews or Gentiles can claim this verse to be applicable in one's life, provided he/she has accepted Jesus Christ as his/her personal Savior.

The power of God keeps us and assures us that we will inherit that kind blessing in heaven that Peter referred to. We will have eternal life and be with the Lord Jesus Christ always. That inheritance is incorruptible, and undefiled. It does not fade away. We may face trials and tribulations in this world, but the rewards that are reserved for us in eternity are great.

"And every man that striveth for the mastery is temperate in all things. Now they do it to obtain a corruptible crown; but we an incorruptible". (1 Corinthians 9:25)

"In a moment, in the twinkling of an eye, at the last trump: for the trumpet shall sound, and the dead shall be raised incorruptible, and we shall be changed". (1 Corinthians 15:52) "Being born again, not of corruptible seed, but of incorruptible, by the word of God, which liveth and abideth for ever" (1 Peter 1:23) We are all sojourners on this earth

Peter, one of the disciples of Jesus Christ, says we are all sojourners on this earth. Our true inheritance, which is incorruptible, and that does not fade away, is in heaven. As aliens on this earth we enjoy all the privileges of citizens, yet our true treasure, that does not perish, is in heaven. Therefore, we should greatly rejoice.

The price paid for us to have this great inheritance is the blood of Jesus Christ on the cross of Calvary. No amount of good works can save a person, and the only way to receive salvation is by the grace of God, through faith in him.

There are only three occasions shown in the Old Testament, when the blood was sprinkled. First one was when a covenant was established (Exodus 24:5-8), the second one was when Aaron and his sons were anointed as priests (Exodus 29:21), and the third one was when an unclean leper was cleansed (Leviticus 14:6-7).

Now, when we apply this to ourselves, New Testament believers, it is so true that a covenant was established with the sprinkling of the blood of Jesus Christ, we are all made priests unto him, and we, who were unclean, are cleansed from our sin. We are saved and made a new creation (2 Corinthians 5:17).

The sacrifice of Jesus Christ bearing our sin upon the cross enabled us to approach the Father in heaven, through His only begotten son, Jesus Christ, who is our mediator. The blood of Jesus cleansed us from our sin. Although our temptations are manifold, yet the trial of our faith is much more precious than that of gold, which perishes. (1 Peter 1st Chapter)

DAY 17 NO MAN SAW GOD

"Jesus saith unto him, Have I been so long time with you, and yet hast thou not known me, Philip? **he** that hath seen me hath seen the Father; and how sayest thou then, Show us the Father?" John 14:9

We love our Lord, not because we are able to see him physically, but because of our belief in him. In 1 John 4:19 we read that 'We love him, because he first loved us'.

Our savior, as described in Song of Solomon 5th Chapter, is 'altogher lovely' and ' white and ruddy, the chiefest among ten thousand'. Yet, it is not the beauty or the physical appearance of our Lord that makes us to love him but because he has shown his love toward us by shedding his precious blood for our sake in order that we may not be condemned but be saved.

This was the way for our redemption from our sin. He is the way, the truth and the life. There is no one, except Jesus, who can save us from the eternal damnation. That is the reason why after having been saved we 'rejoice with joy unspeakable and full of glory'.

We have received salvation of our souls by faith in him and the efficacy of his blood shed for us, rather than any works associated with law. Our salvation is not by any good works that we do or have done, but it is by believing in him through faith. The Old Testament prophets have enquired about this salvation.

They prophesied about the grace and about the salvation that will be available through the only begotten Son of God. They prophesied about the sufferings of Jesus and the glory that he would have thereafter. Although they prophesied about these things, yet these were reserved for us to hear about and believe. The angels desired to look into these things, but it was for us to have that privilege to hear and believe. The gospel of Jesus Christ is preached unto us, and it is great privilege for those who hear the good news about Jesus Christ to accept his sacrifice on the cross for our sake.

Peter asks us to gird up the loins of our minds, be sober and hope for the grace that is to be brought unto us at the revelation of Jesus Christ. He asks us to follow Jesus who was holy and be as obedient children.

We should neither lust nor live in fashion with an idea of attracting the other gender into lustful thoughts. Our conversation should bring glory and honor unto our Lord Jesus. (1 Peter 1:8-17) "The Price is already paid for" John 19:30

When Jesus therefore had received the vinegar, he said, It is finished: and he bowed his head, and gave up the ghost.

This is one of the seven sayings of Jesus when he was on the cross of Calvary. He was despised and rejected by man

This is the fulfillment of prophesy that is written in Isaiah 53:4-7 "Surely he hath borne our griefs, and carried our sorrows: yet we did esteem him stricken, smitten of God, and afflicted. But he was wounded for our transgressions, he was bruised for our iniquities: the chastisement of our peace was upon him; and with his stripes we are healed.

All we like sheep have gone astray; we have turned everyone to his own way; and the LORD hath laid on him the iniquity of us all. He was oppressed, and he was afflicted, yet he opened not his mouth: he is brought as a lamb to the slaughter, and as a sheep before her shearers is dumb, so he openeth not his mouth".

He was led like a lamb to be slaughtered. His hands and feet were nailed. He was numbered with the transgressors his death.

Isaiah 53:10 "Yet it pleased the LORD to bruise him; he hath put him to grief: when thou shalt make his soul an offering for sin, he shall see his seed, he shall prolong his days, and the pleasure of the LORD shall prosper in his hand." His blood was paid as price for our redemption. There was nothing more, nor is anything more to be done any person for receiving salvation. It is just the faith in him as Lord and Savior is the requirement to have everlasting life.

Jesus took upon himself our infirmities and sin so that we may have everlasting life by accepting as our Lord. It pleased the Father to bruise him so that we may receive salvation. There is no price attached to that invaluable gift that is made available for us.

The price is already paid. If we call on the Father, He will help us that we pass our pilgrimage on this earth in fear of Him, rendering to Him His due worship inasmuch as we are not redeemed with silver or gold, but by the blood of His only begotten Son Jesus Christ, whom John identified as the Lamb of God, who takes away the sin. Peter confirms that this Lamb of God, Lord Jesus was without blemish and without spot.

The Father in heaven judges every man according to his/her works while sojourning on this earth. He keeps record of our vain conversations that we may have received from our earthly fathers following traditions.

Therefore, let us keep in mind that as the Scripture says, Lord Jesus Christ was 'foreordained before the foundation of the world' and he was revealed unto us in the form of man, died upon the cross, bearing our sins, so that we may have redemption from sin, and whom God raised him from the dead on the dead after crucifixion.

Jesus is not dead lying in the grave just as anybody on this earth was born, but he was raised from the dead on the third day as prophesied, on the third day and later after forty days on this earth, ascended into heaven. He is now seated on the right hand of the Majesty, pleading on our behalf with the Father. Our faith in God increases as our days pass on this earth because of this infallible truth.

Our souls are purified by believing on this truth and hope increases as our sojourning on this earth tapers to start afresh eternal life with the only one, who paid the price for our salvation. Likewise, our love for one another should be fervent and pure. Just as grass withers, and flower fades, our life on this earth is also temporal and temporary, but the life with Jesus is eternal as the Word of God endures for ever Does God forget His promises

'Go, and gather the elders of Israel together, and say unto them, The LORD God of your fathers, the God of Abraham, of Isaac, and of Jacob, appeared unto me, saying, I have surely visited you, and seen that which is done to you in Egypt: And I have said, I will bring you up out of the affliction of Egypt unto the land of the Canaanites, and the Hittites, and the Amorites, and the Perizzites, and the Hivites, and the Jebusites, unto a land flowing with milk and honey. And they shall hearken to thy voice: and thou shalt come, thou and the elders of Israel, unto the king of Egypt, and ye shall say unto him, The LORD God of the Hebrews hath met with us: and now let us go, we beseech thee, three days' journey into the wilderness, that we may sacrifice to the LORD our God. (Exodus 3:16-18)'.

It seemed as if God has forgotten the children of Israel and His promises to them when they were under the bondage of slavery under Pharaoh for nearly four hundred years. God made a covenant with Abraham that he and his posterity through Isaac will be blessed and will become great nation.

Indeed, God was at work when the children of Israel were under the bondage of Pharaoh, disciplining them, multiplying them. Then when it was time God said to Moses, that He heard the cry of the children of Israel, and would deliver them. He has spoken to Moses in clear terms as to how he should ask Pharaoh to let them go so that they can go yonder and worship their God.

Pharaoh refused to let them go; but after ten plagues were brought upon the land of Egypt, he finally let the children of Israel go. On their way to Canaan, the children of Israel defeated six nations and thirty one kings. Pharisees tried to trap Jesus with their questions

Quoting Scriptures just as the tempter did the Scriptures when he tested Jesus (Matt 4th Ch.), Pharisees and Sadducees, highly educated elite and religious leaders of Jesus's time attempted to trap Jesus several times by the words. One such attempt was by quoting from Deuteronomy 25:5-10 about the law of Moses, and said to Jesus, that according to law, 'if a man die having no children his brother shall marry his wife and raise up seed unto his brother'.

Their attempt was to take advantage of this scripture and posed a question to him that if seven brothers attempt in vain to raise an offspring from a single woman, whose wife would she be in resurrection. (Matt. 22:24-30)

Jesus understood their motif and replied to them that they do err in being unaware of scriptures and the power of God. He said, 'But as touching the resurrection of the dead, have ye not read that which was spoken unto you by God, saying, I am the God of Abraham, and the God of Isaac, and the God of Jacob? God is not the God of the dead, but of the living' Matthew 22:31-32. Further, He said that in resurrection no one will marry nor anyone is given in marriage, but they all will be like angels in heaven.

Sadducees then tried to trap Jesus in another question. One of them was a lawyer, who asked him as to which commandment in the law was great. Jesus answered and said to them, 'Thou shalt love the Lord thy God with all thy heart, and with all thy soul, and with all thy mind. This is the first and great commandment. And the second is like unto it, Thou shalt love thy neighbour as thyself. On these two commandments hang all the law and the prophets'.

Jesus, knowing their thoughts and intentions said to them that he has not come to destroy law or the prophets but to fulfill. He also said that the law and the prophets were until John and then onward 'the kingdom of God is preached'.

Warning them, Jesus said that the deeds and works, which they consider as righteousness in their own eyes according to their own understanding does not save them. They, who try to justify themselves before men, but God knows their hearts and judges them. They consider themselves as highly esteemed but they are abomination in the sight of God. (Luke 16:15-17). Jesus affirmed that heaven and hearth will pass but one title of the law will not fail.

Jesus asked them why were they angry at him when he healed a man on Sabbath, while they who profess Sabbath should be a day of rest fail to observe that day and circumcise on that day. Is it not worth considering the fact that 'In the end of the sabbath, as it began to dawn toward the first day of the week, came Mary Magdalene and the other Mary to see the sepulcher'. Matthew 28:1 The Sabbath was over, and on the first day of the week, Jesus rose from the dead. Jesus also said 'For the Son of man is Lord even of the sabbath day' Matthew 12:8

DAY 18 OUR BLESSINGS IN ABRAHAM

"And he said unto him, I am the LORD that brought thee out of Ur of the Chaldees, to give thee this land to inherit it" (Genesis 15:7)

Abraham's name was "Abram" before he was renamed by God as "Abraham".

A covenant is a mutual agreement between two parties and it is deemed to have agreed upon when both the parties pass between the divided pieces of an animal that are laid against each other indicating that if any one of the party breaks the covenant his body would suffer the same kind of death as the animal suffered. There are two types of covenants recorded in the Bible and they are

Conditional and
Unconditional

The covenant that God made with Abraham was Unconditional. The LORD said to Abram to take an heifer of three years old, a she goat of three years old, a ram of three years old, turtle dove and a young pigeon and divide them in the midst and lay each piece one against another. Abram did as the LORD commanded him. He did not divide birds and when the fowls came down on the carcasses, he drove them away (Ref. Genesis 15:7-11)

As the dusk started growing a deep sleep fell upon Abram and lo, a horror of great darkness fell upon him. The LORD spoke to

Abram in his sleep and said to be sure that His seed shall be stranger in the land that is not theirs and shall serve the nation which will afflict them for four hundred years and that the LORD will judge that nation.

As a seal affixed to the covenant by the LORD the burning lamp of the LORD passed between those pieces. It may be noted here that Abram did not pass between the divided pieces which clearly indicates that it was one sided agreement.

In the same day the LORD made a covenant with Abram that He gave the land to him from the river of Egypt unto the great river, the river Euphrates; this land is commonly called as the "fertile crescent". Obviously, as seen in the Scriptures the word of the LORD with regard to their bondage of slavery was fulfilled when the children of Israel served Pharaoh of Egypt for four hundred years and, thereafter, God judged Pharaoh and Egypt.

The covenant that was made between God and Moses was conditional, that is to say, if they did what the LORD said to them, then God would do what He promised to them. However, the covenant that the LORD made with Abram was one sided, that is, the LORD made the covenant with Abram and He will fulfill His covenant no matter what the seed of Abram would do. God's promise will never fail and He will not go back on anyone of His promises. The LORD's covenant with Abram was from the LORD and He did not put a condition to fulfill His promise. (Ref. Genesis Chapter 15)

The LORD said to Abram as we read in Genesis Chapter 17 that he shall circumcise the flesh of his foreskin and it shall be a token of the covenant. He also said that every male of eight days old shall be circumcised among his people. Whoever did not obey this command of the LORD was cut off from the lineage of Abram but still the covenant the LORD made with

Abram was not treated as abrogated. The LORD's Promise still stands to be fulfilled in the lives of the descendants of Abraham. The LORD gave privilege to those who are bought with money by Abram and his descendants to reap the blessings of Abram when they are circumcised and otherwise they do not. (Ref. Genesis 17:11-14)

New Testament believer can be sure that it is not by keeping the Law of Moses that the promises are inherited but by the promise that the LORD made to Abraham (Cf. Galatians 4:7, Romans 8:17, Romans 10:17, Ephesians 2:8)

"For if the inheritance be of the law, it is no more of promise: but God gave it to Abraham by promise" (Galatians 3:18)

"For with the heart man believeth unto righteousness; and with the mouth confession is made unto salvation" (Romans 10:10)

DAY 19 THE EMBLEMS

"And he took bread, and gave thanks, and brake it, and gave unto them, saying, This is my body which is given for you: this do in remembrance of me". (Luke 22:19)

Lord Jesus Christ was scourged and was insulted with crown of thorns on His head. A superscription which read as "THIS IS JESUS THE KING OF THE JEWS" was set up over his head. He was the Messiah but Jews did not realize the fact; rather they mocked Him and crucified on the cross. To add up to the insult they crucified the righteous and innocent Jesus in the midst of two others who were thieves.

Yet, it pleased the Father to bruise Him for our sake and for three long dark hours our sin that Lord Jesus was bearing on behalf of us was judged on the cross. It was at this time that He cried with loud voice "Eli, Eli Lama Sabakthani" which means "My God, my God why have you forsaken me". It was the only one occasion when the Son addressed His Father as "My God, my God" because the Father forsook Him during the period when our sin on Jesus was being judged.

Some believe that the bread and the wine will transform to the actual body of Christ and His blood although the bread and the wine retain their original appearance, odor, and taste.

"Then Jesus said unto them, Verily, verily, I say unto you, Except ye eat the flesh of the Son of man, and drink his blood, ye have no life in you. Whoso eateth my flesh, and drinketh my blood, hath eternal life; and I will raise him up at the last day" (John 6:53-54)

In essence we worship Lord Jesus Christ in spirit and in truth with all our heart, and with all our soul with all our mind. It is not the bread and the wine in the cup that deserve our worship but the one who gave them to us to remember Him. The bread and the wine in the cup do not transform to the actual body and blood of Jesus but they are emblems that we take and by eating and drinking of them we remember His crucifixion. Belief that these emblems turn to the actual body and blood of Jesus Christ is equivalent to believing that Jesus was re-crucified; and we never want to crucify Jesus repeatedly.

"It is the spirit that quickeneth; the flesh profiteth nothing: the words that I speak unto you, they are spirit, and they are life" (John 6:63)

The meaning behind looking at the brazen serpent was lost very quickly when the children of Israel worshipped it and made an idol of it. King Hezekiah removed during his period the high places, broke the images and cut down the groves and broke in pieces the serpent that Moses had made because the children of Israel burnt incense to it. It is sad that many turn Lord's supper into idolatry rather than remembering the crucifixion of Jesus who died for us only once and did not or does not die repeatedly.

"Who needeth not daily, as those high priests, to offer up sacrifice, first for his own sins, and then for the people's: for this he did once, when he offered up himself" (Hebrews 7:27)

"By the which will we are sanctified through the offering of the body of Jesus Christ once for all". (Hebrews 10:10)

We are asked to remember the Lord Jesus Christ's death as often as we can. Lord Jesus Christ suffered death on behalf of us. He was buried and His body did not suffer corruption. He was raised on the third day and appeared unto many for forty days and then He ascended into heaven. He is now seated on the right hand of the Majesty and pleading on our behalf. He is coming back soon and we are given the hope of seeing Him when He comes again in the clouds. We, the believers in Christ, will be with Him for ever and ever.

"For Christ also hath once suffered for sins, the just for the unjust, that he might bring us to God, being put to death in the flesh, but quickened by the Spirit" (1 Peter 3:18)

DAY 20 DAVID'S GRATITUDE

One of the best thanksgiving Psalms by David is Psalm 116. From the low ebb of his life he rises and not only he gives thanks but he also advises his soul and others to continue to give thanks to God.

There was reason for David to give thanks to God. The LORD chose him to be the king over Israel even when he was a boy looking after his sheep. It was not until King Saul was removed from his throne by God that David possessed the crown to rule Israel, nor did David make haste to remove Saul from his kingship. He waited upon the LORD for many years and when it was God's time he accepted kingship and took over to reign over Israel. David was king over whole Israel and its people. His first victory even before he became king was when he killed Philistine Giant Goliath when he was a boy of 12.

In all David's victories over his enemies God was with him. Yet, when he committed sin God did not spare him and He said that the sword shall not depart from his house. God forgave David' sin but did not spare him from paying its price even though he asked for forgiveness for the sin he committed with Bathsheba and the conspiracy he devised to kill her husband Uriah. He had to see unwanted pregnancy in her; his first child was dead; his own son Absalom pursued him to kill. He was defeated once for numbering his army that which was not pleasing to the LORD. Yet in all these times God did not leave him comfortless. In spite of all these God said David was a man after His own heart. David was right with God and he kept commandments and statutes of the LORD.

David cried to the LORD in times of his needs and God answered his prayers. He was thankful always to the LORD for the mercies he received from Him. He acknowledged that the LORD heard his voice not because of his merits but because of His love and, therefore, he loved Him. He continued to sing that the LORD inclined his ear unto him and heard his prayers. He says, therefore, that he will call upon the LORD as long as he lives. He said in other times...

"In the LORD put I my trust: how say ye to my soul, Flee as a bird to your mountain?" (Psalms 11:1)

"For thou wilt not leave my soul in hell; neither wilt thou suffer thine Holy One to see corruption" (Psalms 16:10)

The thanksgiving that he offered to the LORD was not just because God did small things to him but because the LORD's hands got under him and lifted him when his death compassed him and when the pains of hell got hold of him. He was relieved from troubles and sorrows and it is then that he called upon the LORD and the LORD answered his prayers.

One such prayer was...

"And now, O LORD God, the word that thou hast spoken concerning thy servant, and concerning his house, establish it for ever, and do as thou hast said" (2 Samuel 7:25)

"Therefore now let it please thee to bless the house of thy servant, that it may continue for ever before thee: for thou, O Lord GOD, hast spoken it: and with thy blessing let the house of thy servant be blessed for ever" (2 Samuel 7:29)

David committed himself to follow the LORD and kept His statutes. When David's son Solomon committed abomination before God the LORD said to him that he did not keep the statutes of the LORD as David his father kept and walked in the ways of the LORD. God rent the kingdom of Solomon into two.

David was blessed and so was his kingdom. He realized how much he was taken care of by the LORD and said...

"What shall I render unto the LORD [for] all his benefits toward me? I will take the cup of salvation, and call upon the name of the LORD. I will pay my vows unto the LORD now in the presence of all his people" Psalm 116:12-14

DAY 21 SUBMIT TO THE WILL OF THE LORD

Matthew Chapter 8 records a series of miracles done by Lord Jesus Christ. In his own words Matthew says that the prophecy was fulfilled in the performance of miracles by Jesus. The healing Jesus brought about on the sick was not only on their physical condition but also on the spiritual condition.

As Isaiah prophesied in chapter 53 He bore our griefs and carried our sorrows. Jesus was fully divine and fully man when He was on this earth. He was born Jew and His first ministry was primarily to His own people. However, His own rejected Him and salvation is given to gentiles. Nevertheless, the healings He brought on people as recorded in Matthew reveal to us some marvelous truths.

The first healing recorded in Matthew Chapter 8 was of healing the leper. According to Jewish law the touching of a leper is prohibited; but Jesus, who was divine, has gone beyond His earthly conditions and touched the leper and healed him. The second healing recorded in the same chapter was on the servant of gentile official. The third was on mother-in-law of His disciple, Peter.

The ways adopted by Jesus in healing the sick were different on different occasions. First it was touching the leper who was suffering from the loathsome disease considered as a sign of sin. The Jewish leper had no social and religious privileges and yet this leper was restored by the compassionate Lord Jesus. The leper was healed and restored based on his prayer and faith. According to Mosaic Law there were specific conditions to be fulfilled in cleansing a leper. However, Jesus, the Lord of all, touched him, healed him and said to him to go to the priest and offer the gift as Mosaic Law demanded in order that it may bear testimony to them.

In the second healing that the Lord brought on the servant of a gentile centurion the word of the Lord was sufficient to heal the servant who was at far distance from the scene where the Centurion was pleading with the Lord. The centurion had great faith and prayed to the Lord to say a word of healing and believed that the word of the Lord was powerful to heal his servant. According to his faith and prayer his request was granted by Lord Jesus Christ.

In the third healing that the Lord brought about was according to His own voluntary will that He exercised in touching the mother-in-law of Peter after seeing her and her condition. She was restored to her normal health and she got up immediately to serve Him and His disciples. It is not known whether or not Peter's mother-in-law had faith or believed, and yet as the record bears witness the healing on her was performed at the behest of the will of Lord Jesus Christ, the Son of God.

Later in the evening of the same day there were many unnamed and unnumbered sick that were brought to the Lord and He had compassion on all of them. There were those who were demon-possessed and there were those who were sick and the Scripture records that Jesus healed all that were sick. It is the sovereign will of God that prevailed and prevails and not as man would expect God to react to their prayers and expectations.

Submit to the Lord that He may exercise His will according to His purposes. In doing so, we will be blessed. God answers prayers. Have faith!

"When the even was come, they brought unto him many that were possessed with devils: and he cast out the spirits with [his] word, and healed all that were sick" Matthew 8:16

DAY 22 THE SONG OF MOSES

"Then sang Moses and the children of Israel this song unto the LORD, and spake, saying, I will sing unto the LORD, for he hath triumphed gloriously: the horse and his rider hath he thrown into the sea" (Exodus Chapter 15:1)

Moses, the servant of God, sang a song unto the LORD as the people of Israel joined him in praising the mighty works of the LORD. Miriam, his sister, Aaron, his brother played timbrel and danced and all the women followed them in playing timbrels and dancing.

Miriam said "...Sing ye to the LORD, for he hath triumphed gloriously; the horse and his rider hath he thrown into the sea". (Exodus 15:21)

After the deliverance of the children of Israel from the mighty and evil forces of Pharaoh the children of Israel and Moses sang the song of praises to the LORD and they sang praises unto the only living God who drowned and killed their enemies in the Red Sea.

The blast from the nostrils of the LORD gathered the waters in the Red sea and it split up to stand upright like heap and with the strength like that of a rock on either side of the dry pathway which the LORD made for the children of Israel and their cattle to tread on.

The outstretched and mighty hand of the LORD delivered them from the bondage of slavery and in recognition of God's faithfulness they sang the song. They sang the excellence of the LORD and praised Him and they sang that the enemy pursued them but they were overthrown by the power of God. The pride of the enemy was brought to no effect and God blew the wind over the Red Sea.

The children of Israel walked to their safety under the mighty hands of God beyond the Red Sea and then at the command of God Moses stretched forth his hand over the Red sea and the sea returned to normal. Egyptians tried to escape against the tide of the waters, but the waters covered the chariots, the horsemen, and the entire host of Pharaoh who came pursuing after them. The LORD took off the wheels of their chariots and His right hand was glorious in power and it dashed the enemy into pieces.

The children of Israel continued singing "Who is like unto thee, O LORD, among the gods? who is like thee, glorious in holiness, fearful in praises, doing wonders?" (Cf. Exodus 15:8, 11, Exodus 13:18-22 and 14:24-30)

The LORD reigns for ever and ever and He is with us always. The Lord never tempts any man and no temptation is greater than the capacity of a man to resist it; rather God provides always a way out to escape from the temptation when he is tempted. Submit to the Lord, be sober, be vigilant, put on His whole armor and resist the wiles of the devil, which comes sometimes like a roaring lion and sometimes like an angel of light.

There is reason for us to sing unto the Lord because Jesus paid price for our salvation. It is neither by silver nor by gold or by our good works but by the precious blood of Jesus that we have our salvation. Let us sing unto the LORD as Psalmist sang unto Him when his heart rejoiced in Him.

"O come, let us sing unto the LORD: let us make a joyful noise to the rock of our salvation" (Psalms 95:1)

DAY 23 SCARLET ROBE AND REED

"And they stripped him, and put on him a scarlet robe. And when they had platted a crown of thorns, they put it upon his head, and a reed in his right hand: and they bowed the knee before him, and mocked him, saying, Hail, King of the Jews!" (Matthew 27:28, 29)

After following the illegal arrest of Jesus, few incidents took place. When it was morning all the chief priests, elders of the people took counsel against Jesus to crucify him. (Matthew 27:1) There is elaborate description about the incidents that took place before his crucifixion. This meditation is about the mockery Jesus faced on behalf of us at the hands of the people who shouted that Jesus should be crucified.

There are three points that need our meditation. One is that they stripped him and put on him a scarlet robe. Second one is about the crown of thorns that they put upon his head. And, the third one is about a reed that they gave in his right hand and insulted him.

There is reason why God instructed Moses to use colors viz. Blue, Scarlet and Purple for curtains in the Tabernacle. The color Scarlet indicates sin and redemption. We claim the promise of redemption as for Israel as it is written in Isaiah 1:18 where it states "Come now, and let us reason together, saith the LORD: though your sins be as scarlet, they shall be as white as snow; though they be red like crimson, they shall be as wool".

The people's desire was to insult Jesus by stripping him and putting on him a scarlet robe (Matthew 27:28). It was divine desire that he bears our sin upon him in order to redeem us from the sin. He paid the price for our sake and bore insult on behalf of us.

Secondly they put on his head a crown of thorns. In the beginning when God created heavens and earth and herbs, plants, animals everything was good. God saw that it was good. In Genesis 1:26 to 31 there is a description as to how God created man in his own image and gave him the authority over every living creature and he saw that it was good. There is no mention anywhere that thorns and thistles were made for man. But when man transgressed God's command, God cursed the earth for man's sake and it started bringing forth thorns and thistles from then onward.

Thorns also and thistles shall it bring forth to you; and you shall eat the plants of the field; (Genesis 3:18)

When people put the crown of thorns on the head of Jesus they exhibited their insult toward him but it was divine purpose that He should bear our curse upon his head on the cross in order that we may be redeemed of that curse.

Thirdly they gave a reed in his right hand and bowed the knee before him and insulted him saying "Hail, King of the Jews"

A reed is common name for many aquatic plants, most of them large grasses with hollow stem or a very weak flexible strip of cane. They gave this grass piece in the right hand of Jesus and insulted him saying "ail, King of the Jews"

Apostle Paul shows the importance of right hand. Speaking about Lord Jesus Christ who is now seated at the right hand of the Father he writes...

"Which he wrought in Christ, when he raised him from the dead, and set him at his own right hand in the heavenly places" (Ephesians 1:20)

Psalmist wrote about right hand of God whom he trusts as the only help and rock of refuge.

"Even there shall thy hand lead me, and thy right hand shall hold me". (Psalm 139:10)

The writer of Hebrews writes about Lord Jesus Christ in Hebrew 1:3 "Who being the brightness of his glory, and the express image of his person, and upholding all things by the word of his power, when he had by himself purged our sins, sat down on the right hand of the Majesty on high"

He writes in Hebrews 1:8 "But unto the Son he saith, Thy throne, O God, is for ever and ever: a sceptre of righteousness is the sceptre of thy kingdom".

Israelites sang a song after crossing the Red Sea. "Thy right hand, O LORD, is become glorious in power: thy right hand, O LORD, hath dashed in pieces the enemy". (Exodus 15:6)

David gave his mother seat on his right hand (Ref: 1 Kings 2:19)

The King of kings, Lord of lords, and the God of gods, Lord Jesus who will be seen sitting on the right hand of power and comes in the clouds of heaven (Matthew 26:54) was seen here bearing a reed in shame in his right hand so that we may not be put to shame. He bore shame for our sake.

Let us be always thankful to our savior Jesus for taking upon himself our sin and bearing insult on our behalf. Let us worship him in spirit and truth

DAY 24 HEZEKIAH DEFEATS SENNACHERIB

Out of twenty kings of the Kingdom of Judah there were only few kings who did that which was right in the sight of the LORD. One of them was king Hezekiah. There was none before him in the history of kings of Judah who trusted and revered the LORD so much as he did. He was twenty five years old when he began to reign and reigned for twenty nine years in Jerusalem. The LORD was with him and he prospered.

"He removed the high places, and brake the images, and cut down the groves, and brake in pieces the brasen serpent that Moses had made: for unto those days the children of Israel did burn incense to it: and he called it Nehushtan" (2 Kings 18:4)

Hezekiah rebelled against King of Assyria and did not serve him and defeated Philistines. In his fourth year of reign Shalmaneser, king of Assyria, attacked Samaria, besieged it took full control of it in two years. He took captive of Israel and moved them to Halah, Habor and to the cities of Medes. The LORD gave them over to King of Assria because they transgressed God's covenant and were disobedient to the Laws given by God through His servant Moses.

Sennacherib, king of Asyria came up against Hezekiah in the fourteenth year of latter's reign and fenced cities of Judah and took them. Lachish was a very strategic city where the armies pitch one against another for war and it is at that city that Sennacherib came and boasted in pride. Hezekiah, king of Judah, was depressed and disappointed and, therefore, sent word of apology that he would take punishment for not serving him. Sennacherib imposed on Hezekiah a fine of three hundred talents of silver and thirty talents of gold, which was huge sum. Hezekiah raised the sum from the house of the Lord, treasures of the king's house and even from the gold from the doors of the Solomon's temple and gave to it king Sennacherib.

It is very strange that a king, who had so much faith in God and who did right in the sight of the LORD and trusted the LORD more than anyone in the Kingdom of Judah did before him, now getting disappointed when faced with some trying situation such as Sennacherib taking over Lachish and cities of Judah. Rightly so, he showed that he was also fallible and human just as any of us.

Elijah, who was so courageous a prophet, once feared Jezebel and ran from her presence to hide himself, but later recovered from that fear when the angel of the LORD comforted him. He heard the voice of the LORD not in strong wind, or in the earthquake, or fire, but in a still small voice that said "What doest thou here, Elijah" and Elijah obeyed the instructions from the LORD (1 Kings 19-4-14)

Likewise, King Hezekiah also recovered from fear and brought Sennacherib to his feet when God helped him consequent upon his praying to the LORD for help. Sennacherib's blasphemous words, arrogant speech came to nothing.

Hezekiah prayed to the LORD saying "O LORD God of Israel, which dwellest between the cherubims, thou art the God, even thou alone, of all the kingdoms of the earth; thou hast made heaven and earth".

The LORD heard prayer of Hezekiah and the angel of the LORD went out and "smote in the camp of the Assyrians an hundred fourscore and five thousand: and when they arose early in the morning, behold, they were all dead corpses". (1 Kings 19:35)

Sennacherib, king of Assyria, went back and lived in Nineveh and worshipped his god, Nisroch and he was killed by his own two sons. (cf. 2 Kings 19:36-37)

"But the LORD is my defence; and my God is the rock of my refuge" (Psalms 94:22)

DAY 25 LEPER HEALED

"And, behold, there came a leper and worshipped him, saying, Lord, if thou wilt, thou canst make me clean. And Jesus put forth his hand, and touched him, saying, I will; be thou clean. And immediately his leprosy was cleansed. And Jesus saith unto him, See thou tell no man; but go thy way, shew thyself to the priest, and offer the gift that Moses commanded, for a testimony unto them" (Matthew 8:2-4)

Leprosy is a sign of sin. Notwithstanding any theory the medical science would say about Leprosy it was under the control of God who turn incurable Leprosy as transient that could be arrested and could turn that which could be arrested to last permanently as He wished. Lord Jesus Christ healed leper fully as we read in Matthew 8:2-4.

A leper approached Lord Jesus Christ and worshipped Him and prayed to him that if He willed He can make clean. The leper believed that Lord Jesus Christ can heal him and, therefore, asserted very firmly that if Lord Jesus Christ willed He can heal him. Seeing how the leper believed in Him, Jesus touched him saying, "I will, be thou clean". The man was fully healed of leprosy immediately and was cleansed. Jesus said to him not to tell anyone but go the priest and offer the gift that Moses commanded for a testimony.

1. The leper worshipped Jesus
2.The leper prayed to Jesus
3. The leper acknowledged the Lordship of Jesus

Worship is to bow down and pay respect. The word is translated from Greek transliterated word "proskuneo". (Strong's number 4352),which means to kiss, like a dog licking his master's hand or to prostrate oneself in homage.

It can be seen that the leper prayed to Jesus that if He willed He can make the leper clean. Why did leper use the word ‘clean’, instead of ‘heal’. Hebrew transliterated word ″tahowr″ (Hebrew Strong’s Number 2889) and Greek transliterated word ″katharizo″ (Strong’s number 2511) mean to cleanse, purge, purify. Obviously leprosy is un-clean, impure, and needs to be purged and cleansed.

There are three things that Jesus told the cleansed leper to do.

Tell No man (Until he sees the priest to show that he was healed of leprosy)
1. Offer the gift to the priest as Moses commanded
2. Bear it as a testimony in order that he may be admitted into society (Cf. Lev 14:1-32)

Lord Jesus Christ came into this world in the form of a servant and in the likeness of man and did many miracles and wonders. He taught repentance and the way to salvation. He said:

″Jesus saith unto him, I am the way, the truth, and the life: no man cometh unto the Father, but by me″ (John 14:6)

Lord Jesus Christ bore our sin that was worse than leprosy disease in order that whoever believes in Him shall not perish but have everlasting life. Whoever repents of his/her sins and confession by mouth that the Lord Jesus Christ is the Son of God and believes that God raised Him from the dead shall be saved.

″That if thou shalt confess with thy mouth the Lord Jesus, and shalt believe in thine heart that God hath raised him from the dead, thou shalt be saved″ (Romans 10:9)

"For he hath made him to be sin for us, who knew no sin; that we might be made the righteousness of God in him" (2 Corinthians 5:21)

DAY 26 FAITH SAVES (Centurion's Servant healed)

"And when Jesus was entered into Capernaum, there came unto him a centurion, beseeching him, And saying, Lord, my servant lieth at home sick of the palsy, grievously tormented. And Jesus saith unto him, I will come and heal him" (Matthew 8:5-7)

The centurion, who approached Jesus to heal His servant, was a gentile from Roman Army. Because it was against the Mosaic Law for a Jew to mix up with Gentile it would have been an awkward situation for Jesus, who was a Jew, to enter Centurion's house. However the Lord said He would go to centurion's house and heal his servant.

God was against the children of Abraham marrying Canaanite women because the latter were idolaters. Such prohibition was present even before Mosaic Law was given. (Cf. Genesis 24:3, Genesis 24:37, Genesis 28:1).

Thereafter, God chose Israel as His nation and the people of Israel as His people. The LORD prohibited Idolatry and, therefore, prohibited mixing up with Canaanites and other nations. However, considering the fact that Moses married a Cushite (Ethiopian) woman, it is evident that God was not angry with inter-racial marriages.

God was against mixing up with Gentiles because they were idolaters and not because they were of different races. God was angry with Solomon because he married women who were idolaters. This obviously shows that even among the children of Israel there were many races. According to Jewish Encyclopedia there was a large population of Ethiopians among Israelites.

Incidentally, centurions were held in very good light in the Scriptures. There are at least five references about Centurions.
1. "And when Jesus was entered into Capernaum, there came unto him a centurion, beseeching him" (Matthew 8:5)
2.. "Now when the centurion, and they that were with him, watching Jesus, saw the earthquake, and those things that were done, they feared greatly, saying, Truly this was the Son of God" (Matthew 27:54)
3. "There was a certain man in Caesarea called Cornelius, a centurion of the band called the Italian band" (Acts 10:1)
4. "But the chief captain Lysias came upon us, and with great violence took him away out of our hands" (Acts 24:7)
5. "And when it was determined that we should sail into Italy, they delivered Paul and certain other prisoners unto one named Julius, a centurion of Augustus' band" (Acts 27:1)

The Centurion, who approached Jesus, realized the awkward situation that the Lord would face and said to Him that he was not worthy that Jesus should go into his house.

He pleaded with Jesus that He may speak the word ordering healing of his servant and trusted that his servant would be healed by the word of Lord Jesus. He knew and trusted in the spiritual authority and power of the word of the Lord. He cited his own authority over his soldiers under him and servant. He said that he could command one to come and another to go and they all, including his servant, will obey his commands.

Lord Jesus Christ would not have been wrong even if He had gone under the roof of centurion's house because He was the Son of God. At one point he said that He was the Lord of the Sabbath. According toe Mosaic Law Sabbath day violator could be killed by stoning.

"For the Son of man is Lord even of the sabbath day" Mat 12:8

Jesus marveled at the faith of the centurion and said to them that followed Him that He did not find so great faith even among Israelites.

Giving utmost importance to faith that saves a person and healing that he/she would receive Jesus said that many shall come from east and from west and sit down with Abraham, and Isaac, and Jacob in the kingdom of heaven, whereas, even the children of Israel may lose that privilege because of their faith in Him.

Lord Jesus Christ then commanded the centurion to go his way and said that his servant was healed and, surely, his servant was healed in the selfsame hour.

"And Jesus said unto the centurion, Go thy way; and as thou hast believed, [so] be it done unto thee. And his servant was healed in the selfsame hour". Matthew 8:13

DAY 27 PETER'S MOTHER-IN-LAW HEALED

"And when Jesus was come into Peter's house, he saw his wife's mother laid, and sick of a fever. And he touched her hand, and the fever left her: and she arose, and ministered unto them" (Matthew 8:14-15)

Jesus healed a leper and Centurion's servant and then went to Peter's house where he saw Peter's mother-in-law laid and sick of a fever. Jesus touched her and the fever left her and she arose and ministered to them.

Even though this is very short narration in the scriptures where it is seen that Jesus healed his disciple's mother-in-law it brings out few interesting thoughts.

1. Can a servant of the Lord be married?
2. Is healing possible?
3. Was any prophecy fulfilled when Jesus healed the sick?

The first thought is:

Peter was an ardent disciple of Lord Jesus Christ and he was a married man. If marriage of any servant of the Lord was prohibited in the Bible, then Peter could not have been His disciple. If the successors of Peter were to lead unmarried life then it would be their personal choice. Imposing conditions that they should be unmarried is not according to Scriptures.

"Marriage is honourable in all, and the bed undefiled: but whoremongers and adulterers God will judge" (Hebrews 13:4)

The second thought is:

We Christians are not immune to sickness but as long as we are in this world in our fleshly bodies we do suffer from sickness; surely the laws of nature apply to us. However, when we pray to God to have mercy on us and heal us from our sickness, He will deliver us from our sickness or heal us with or without medicines. The healing is purely according to His plan, His will and if it is for His glory.

When God allows persistent sickness in us or when we do not receive healing it is essential that we realize that He has different plan for us and His ways are always good for us who believe in Him. Faith in God does not prohibit us seeking medical help or medicines. Paul advised Timothy once

"Drink no longer water, but use a little wine for thy stomach's sake and thine often infirmities" (1 Timothy 5:23). It was not a recurring solution, of course!

Apostle Paul was apprehensive of his possible glorification by others over the Lord who sent him and affirms that there was given to him a thorn in his flesh, whatever it was, and he called it as 'messenger of Satan' to strike blow on him constantly in order that he might not exalt above measure. He besought the Lord thrice that it might depart from him but notice the reply he received from the Lord and how he consoles himself.

"And he said unto me, My grace is sufficient for thee: for my strength is made perfect in weakness. Most gladly therefore will I rather glory in my infirmities, that the power of Christ may rest upon me" (2 Corinthians 12:9)

The third thought is:

After healing Peter's mother-in-law Jesus healed many that were possessed with devils and those who were sick. Matthews, the Gospel writer, records that prophecy of Isaiah was fulfilled.

"That it might be fulfilled which was spoken by Esaias the prophet, saying, Himself took our infirmities, and bare our sicknesses" (Matthew 8:17)

It was not only true for spiritual healing but for physical healing as well. Isaiah's prophecy says:

"Surely he hath borne our griefs, and carried our sorrows: yet we did esteem him stricken, smitten of God, and afflicted. But he was wounded for our transgressions, he was bruised for our iniquities: the chastisement of our peace was upon him; and with his stripes we are healed". (Isaiah 53:4-5)

DAY 28 DO NOT BE AFRAID

"And fear not them which kill the body, but are not able to kill the soul: but rather fear him which is able to destroy both soul and body in hell" (Matthew 10:28)

Very often man thinks that he is facing temptations beyond his capacity could endure them; but the word of God says that there is no temptation which is not common to man and God is faithful not to allow us to be tempted beyond our capacity. He will also provide a way for us to escape from such temptations and anything beyond is our willful falling into sin (Ref. 1 Corinthians 10:13)

Bible says God does not tempt anyone but He will surely test His children to make them as perfect as man could possibly become.

"Let no man say when he is tempted, I am tempted of God: for God cannot be tempted with evil, neither tempteth he any man" (James 1:13)

It was according to the plan of the LORD that the children of Israel journeyed through the way of the wilderness of the Red Sea instead of going though the way of the land of Philistines; although the latter was nearer route to the Promised Land.

God allowed them not to go through the land of Philistines because the children of Israel, who were slaves in Egypt for more than four hundred years, would prefer to return to Egypt in fear when they face the wars while passing through the lands of other nations (Ref. Exodus 13:17-18).

Later when they came to Kadesh-barnea, which was close to the Promised Land they decided to send spies to search out the Promised Land. God had already told them that the land was given to them but when they insisted on spying out the land He gave them over to their desire and chastised them by allowing them to wander in the wilderness for forty years before their next generation led by Joshua and Caleb possessed the land.

"Behold, the LORD thy God hath set the land before thee: go up and possess it, as the LORD God of thy fathers hath said unto thee; fear not, neither be discouraged" (Deuteronomy 1:21)

How apt it is that when we find ourselves in longer route we usually do not recognize as to why the Lord is not leading us by the nearest route until we see the end result which will be for good for those who believe in Him. Paul writes:

"And we know that all things work together for good to them that love God, to them who are the called according to his purpose" (Romans 8:28)

When the children of Israel were at the Red Sea they were afraid. They saw the sea in front of them and behind them Pharaoh's army, his chariots and horses. They thought they would die either way. If they proceeded further they would die in the Red Sea and if they did not, then Pharaoh's army would capture them and make them slaves again or kill them in the wilderness. However, Moses encouraged them saying, "...Fear ye not, stand still, and see the salvation of the LORD..." (Exodus 14:13) and he continued saying:

"The LORD shall fight for you, and ye shall hold your peace". (Exodus 14:14)

The LORD overthrew the Egyptians in the midst of the Red Sea. When the people of Israel saw that they are saved by the miracle that the LORD did they believed in God and Moses, the servant of the LORD, (Ref. Exodus 14:22-31)

"And we know that all things work together for good to them that love God, to them who are the called according to his purpose". (Romans 8:28)

DAY 29 IT IS FINISHED

"When Jesus therefore had received the vinegar, he said, It is finished: and he bowed his head, and gave up the ghost" John 19:30.

This is one of the seven sayings of Jesus when he was on the cross of Calvary and it was fulfillment of prophecy. He was despised and rejected by men

"Surely he hath borne our griefs, and carried our sorrows: yet we did esteem him stricken, smitten of God, and afflicted. But he was wounded for our transgressions, he was bruised for our iniquities: the chastisement of our peace was upon him; and with his stripes we are healed. All we like sheep have gone astray; we have turned everyone to his own way; and the LORD hath laid on him the iniquity of us all. He was oppressed, and he was afflicted, yet he opened not his mouth: he is brought as a lamb to the slaughter, and as a sheep before her shearers is dumb, so he openeth not his mouth". Isaiah 53:4-7

He was led like a lamb to be slaughtered. His hands and feet were nailed. He was numbered with the transgressors his death.

"Yet it pleased the LORD to bruise him; he hath put him to grief: when thou shalt make his soul an offering for sin, he shall see his seed, he shall prolong his days, and the pleasure of the LORD shall prosper in his hand." Isaiah 53:10

His blood was paid as price for our redemption. There was nothing more, nor is anything more to be done any person for receiving salvation. It is just the faith in him as Lord and Savior is the requirement to have everlasting life. Jesus took upon himself our infirmities, and sin so that we may have everlasting life by accepting as our Lord. It pleased the Father to bruise Him so that we may receive salvation. There is no price attached to that invaluable gift that is made available for us freely.

"Forasmuch as ye know that ye were not redeemed with corruptible things, [as] silver and gold, from your vain conversation [received] by tradition from your fathers; But with the precious blood of Christ, as of a lamb without blemish and without spot" 1 Peter 1:18, 19

The price for our salvation is already paid for. All that a person needs to do is to confess by mouth that Jesus is the Lord and believe in heart that He was raised from the dead. Today is the day of salvation; repent of your sins to the Lord and He forgives them.

DAY 30 THE TRUTH SHALL SET YOU FREE

"And ye shall know the truth, and the truth shall make you free". (John 8:32)

The first few verses from John Chapter 8 describe how a woman, who was caught red handedly in the act of prostitution, was brought by Scribes and Pharisees before Jesus, tempting him to determine whether or not she should be punished as per the Law of Moses. But Jesus stooped down and wrote something on the ground as if he did not hear them. (John 8:6) But when they continued asking him he said to them they may cast stones at her to kill her, but only the man who has never committed any sin in his life may cast first stone at her. None of the accusers threw stones at her and everyone started leaving one by one. Jesus did not condemn the woman and let her go. Scribes and Pharisees still remained there to drag Jesus into debate and catch him on some point and accuse him.

Then Jesus said to Scribes and Pharisees that he was the light of the world and whoever followed him had the light of life and will not walk in darkness. The Pharisees therefore accused him of his birth. When Jesus said to them that He was not alone but he and the Father were one, they did not understand him. They even asked him where his father was. Jesus told them that the record he bore was true and they knew him not fully well. (John 8:14-15). Jesus was born of the Virgin Mary. Luke 1:35 records... "And the angel answered and said unto her, The Holy Ghost shall come upon thee, and the power of the Highest shall overshadow thee: therefore also that holy thing which shall be born of thee shall be called the Son of God". Jesus is the Son of

God.

Jesus said to them that if they knew God they would have known him as well. The argument went on and Pharisees called names and said that he was Samaritan and he had a devil in him. Jesus said that he had no devil in him and they dishonored him but he honored his Father. (John 8:48-50) They did not believe him even though he spoke the Truth.

It can be seen that Jesus was very bold and point blank to give replies to them. Jesus tells them that they need to be freed of their sin. Scribes and Pharisees boasted in themselves that they are the children of Abraham and they were never under bondage that they should be freed from their sin. They did not remember or were ignorant that their forefathers were in bondage of slavery under Pharaoh in Egypt; they did not remember or were ignorant that they were under the bondage of Assyrians and Babylonians. Currently when they were talking to Jesus and as they were trying to trap Jesus on some question and they were already under the bondage of Roman Government. Yet, Jesus was making a point that they were under the bondage of sin and they need to be freed of their sin. Scribes and Pharisees did not realize that Jesus was the Messiah and he was the Son of God. They were claiming that God is their Father and Jesus had to tell them bluntly that their father was devil because they could not recognize the Son of God nor could understand his speech. He said their father, who is the devil, was a murderer from the beginning and lived not in the truth because there is no truth in him. (John 8:41-44)

Jesus spoke the truth because He is the Way, He is the Truth and He is the Light. The Pharisees and Scribes lost their patience and were about to harm Jesus. Even as Jesus was speaking these words many believed; yet Scribes and Pharisees went on accusing him and tried to lay hands on him. The time was net yet come, and therefore, no one could do anything to Jesus and he walked away from their midst unharmed.

DAY 31 GREAT COMMISSION

Pass the message on:

Matthew 28:19-20 'Go ye therefore, and teach all nations, baptizing them in the name of the Father, and of the Son, and of the Holy Ghost: Teaching them to observe all things whatsoever I have commanded you: and, lo, I am with you alway, even unto the end of the world. Amen'.

Before his ascension Lord Jesus commanded his disciples that the message of salvation be proclaimed so that those, who are drawn by the Father may come to him.

Jesus commanded that they should teach all nations, baptize them in the name of the Father, and of the Son, and of the Holy Ghost. He also commanded them that they should teach to observe all things that Jesus commanded them. He did not leave them as orphans in the proclamation of the Gospel, but assured that he will be with them always even unto the end of the world.

Many a time, those who work for Lord Jesus Christ and proclaim the Gospel desire to see immediate results, but they may not see the results. It is the work of the Holy Spirit to convict the sinner of his/her guilt and it is the Father, who draws them unto Him. Noah preached for one hundred years and did not see any results. All that he saw was that he and his own relatives were saved when they entered into the Ark. The Ark had only one door, and that door was the door of salvation. Jesus said that he was the door and no one can come to him unless the Father draws unto him.

John 6:44 'No man can come to me, except the Father which

hath sent me draw him: and I will raise him up at the last day'. The question is if The Father draws someone and it is the only way for anyone to come to the knowledge of salvation, should man preach the Gospel? The answer is surely yes. It is the commandment of Lord Jesus Christ that it is the bounden duty of everyone who has accepted Lord Jesus Christ as his/her personal savior to work for Him and bring forth fruit unto Him.

We need to do our role of working for the Lord, and it is the work of the Holy Spirit to do the rest. We cannot make any excuses that it is the work of the Lord and, therefore, we could keep silence; no! We should work for him and bring glory to His name. Jesus Christ is the Son of God and very God Himself. Jesus said, in John 10:30 'I and my Father are one'.

He said in John 16:15 'All things that the Father hath are mine: therefore said I, that he shall take of mine, and shall shew it unto you'. He said in John 17:11 'And now I am no more in the world, but these are in the world, and I come to thee. Holy Father, keep through thine own name those whom thou hast given me, that they may be one, as we are'.

Apostle Paul wrote about Jesus Christ in Colossians 1:15-18 'Who is the image of the invisible God, the firstborn of every creature: For by him were all things created, that are in heaven, and that are in earth, visible and invisible, whether they be thrones, or dominions, or principalities, or powers: all things were created by him, and for him: And he is before all things, and by him all things consist. And he is the head of the body, the church: who is the beginning, the firstborn from the dead; that in all things he might have the preeminence. Saddducees did not believe in Resurrection

Peter and John, the disciples of Jesus Christ, preached the Gospel and the resurrection from the dead. They healed an impotent man in the name of Jesus. Their ministry was blessed and the number of believers increased from three thousand to five thousand. This kind of preaching, and miracles, in the name of Jesus, grieved the high priest Annas, Caiphas, John, and Alexander, who thought that the preaching belonged to them.

Pharisees believed that keeping law and doing good works can save them, while Sadducees did not believe in the resurrection, and as they were against these teachings they laid hands on Peter and John, the disciples of Jesus, for a trial the next day.

The elders, scribes, Annas, the high priest and high priest's kindred gathered at Jerusalem and questioned the authority by which they preached the resurrection from the dead and healed the impotent man. Peter, then, filled with Holy Spirit, spoke to them and said to them very firmly that they preached and healed the impotent man in the name of Jesus Christ of Nazareth, whom they crucified, and whom God raised from the dead.

Jesus is the stone, who these elders, Pharisees, Sadducees rejected, but God set him as the Chief corner stone. David prophesied about Jesus, who was the stone, that the builders rejected, yet the LORD made him the head stone of the corner.

Peter and John, the disciples of Jesus, who walked with him, witnessed that Jesus was the stone, whom the Jews rejected, but he became the head stone of the corner. They affirm that there is no other name under heaven where anyone can find salvation.

One may object to this preaching but the Bible says it very firmly that there is no salvation except by believing that Jesus is the Savior. Peter and John, the Apostles, who were not learned, or educated, boldly said these things because they were with Jesus and took knowledge from him, who is the only begotten Son of God. The accusers attempted to execute the disciples of Jesus but did not find any cause to punish them, and let them go.

Acts 4:1-14, Ps 118:21-23. Isa. 28:16, Rom 9:33, Eph. 2:20, 1Pet 2:7 Who, being in the form of God, thought it not robbery to be equal with God Phil.2:6

Jesus became poor for us even though he was rich in his glory and was with the Father from eternity. He said he is the beginning and he is the end; he is the Alpha and Omega. He is the creator of this universe, he owns everything, every creation and he is the King of kings, he is the Lord or lords, and he is the God of gods.

Lord Jesus was in the form of God and did not think it robbery to be to equal with God, but made himself of no repute, took the form of servant, and became like a man and dwelt among us. He was born of the Virgin Mary, by the works of Holy Spirit, and was laid in a manger. He was raised in a poor family. His earthly parents offered turtle doves as offerings (Luke 2:24), which was a provision made for poor and those, who could not offer bull or goat as sacrifice as per Old Testament Law. In Colossians 1st Chapter verses 15 to 17, there is a clear description that Jesus is the creator. He is the image of the invisible God, the first born of every creature, and by him were all things created; yet we see that he took the form of man for our sake. He testified, in Luke 9:58 how poor he was on this earth.

All this was took place because Jesus became a sacrifice on our behalf, when he took upon himself, our curse, our sin and shed his precious blood upon the cross of Calvary. The salvation is received by his 'grace' through faith in him that he died and rose for our sake, and by accepting his as 'Lord'. He offered himself on the cross so that we may have riches in him. The earthly riches are not true riches.

What if a man earns whole earth his soul? We are saved by his precious blood and not of any of our works. We are not purchased by gold and/or silver, but by the blood of Jesus, who paid it as price for our salvation. Paul Admonishes Galatians

Apostle Paul admonishes Galatians in no uncertain terms for believing in works associated with salvation. The word he used is 'bewitched'. He was not only asking them as to who has cast a spell over their understanding or enchantment, or fascinated them about their belief that law would save them and works were associated with their salvation, but called them 'fools' (Galatians 3:1) for such belief as they hold that law and works could save them.

The word 'fools' used here does not demean them that they lack wisdom and prudence, but he demeans their misunderstanding that they must do something under the law to God in recompense to what he has done for us. The meaning of 'fool' here was similar to what Jesus meant in Matthew 7:26.

The whole chapter of Galatians 3 deals with this subject of law verses grace. He not only questions them if there is anyone in the world, who is perfect in flesh, but also provides answers to his questions that no one could be saved by the law and works associated with it. He goes on to say that only faith in Jesus Christ, who redeemed us from the curse of the law, could save us.

Abraham believed God, and it was reckoned unto him as righteousness. He says that the children, who are of faith, are the children of Abraham. The Scriptures foresaw that God would justify the heathen through faith, and made available to us, the Word, through preaching, and made available this preaching even before the proclamation of the gospel unto Abraham that in him shall all nations be blessed. Obviously, this indicates that those, who are of faith in Christ, are blessed with faithful Abraham.

Apostle goes on, further, saying that those, who, think that they are still under the works of the law, subject themselves to be under the curse, inasmuch as it written in the Scriptures that whoever continues to believe in becoming perfect by obedience to the commandments written in the law is cursed; no one can be justified before God under the law. The just shall live by faith and it is certain that the law is not of faith, but whosoever, tries to believe that law would save them would live by them, and would be under the curse.

Lord Jesus indeed came for his own, but when they rejected him, salvation was made available for Gentiles; no doubt this was in the plan of God, and this mystery was revealed in Romans11:6-11. He came into this world to provide a way out from these stringent laws, and provided a way for everyone, that by faith in him a person is saved by grace.

Jesus was hung on the cross and bore our sins so that we may not be cursed. It is written that 'cursed is everyone that hangeth on a tree'. He came into this world so that the blessing of Abraham would be available for Gentiles through him, so that the gentiles also may receive the promise of the Spirit through faith.

www.ingramcontent.com/pod-product-compliance
Lightning Source LLC
LaVergne TN
LVHW020716110826
845149LV00012B/2287
9780990780113